"You are a prisoner of the People's National Liberation Front..."

For the next hour I watched the morning begin to break. When I saw how thick the fog was, my heart sank. I must have dozed off again, but at seven o'clock or so I woke up to see an enemy soldier standing directly above me, but he didn't see me. He walked a few feet along the top of the dike, turned around and walked past me again, but at the last second he spotted me, excitedly turned his AK-47 rifle on me, and motioned for me to get up. I tried, but the crash had hurt my back and knees, and spending the night in the mud had left me even stiffer. I tried to stand but slid back down, then struggled to get to my feet. Any thought of trying to resist evaporated when I caught sight of three other NVA soldiers within twenty feet. I finally managed to stand and put my hands above my head. My captor handed me a card printed in English: "You are a prisoner of the People's National Liberation Front. You will not be harmed. You will be humanely treated. If you show progress, you may be released."

I read the card, but its full meaning did not sink in. They were English words, but my mind had gone numb. Through the fog I could hear choppers in the distance not far away, but that distance was now like a million miles away.

WHY DIDN'T YOU GET ME OUT?

A POW's Nightmare in Vietnam

FRANK ANTON

with Tommy Denton

St. Martin's Paperbacks

Previously published by Anton Publishing

WHY DIDN'T YOU GET ME OUT?: A POW'S NIGHTMARE IN VIETNAM

Library of Congress Catalog Card Number: 97-4897

ISBN: 0-312-97488-4

Printed in the United States of America

Anton Publishing hardcover edition published in 1997
St. Martin's Paperbacks edition / June 2000

10 9 8 7 6 5 4 3 2 1

For Jane

WHY DIDN'T YOU GET ME OUT?

Contents

Preface

Nothing fully prepares a young man to go to war, but every soldier carries with him some expectations, or at least preconceptions, about what is expected of him and what he expects from the government that has sent him into battle. As a young helicopter pilot who arrived in Vietnam in April 1967, I quickly encountered the excitement, tragedy, and horror that are the essence of the war. After having been shot down twice without injury and after facing the stark reality many times of being the target of enemy fire, I realized just how tenuous and precious life had become. I had prepared myself for the possibility of being wounded and possibly even being killed. What I had not been prepared for, or had somehow refused to allow myself to consider, was being captured as a prisoner of war.

Flying hair-raising missions as aircraft commander of a UH-1 Huey gunship in the central highlands of the former South Vietnam brought me time and again into the hellish maelstrom of a faraway jungle war where our allies were often unreliable, and our enemy was maddeningly invisible, cunning, and deadly. Somehow, through it all, I was fortunate to escape hundreds of bullets that chewed into the choppers I was flying, and in a sense I began to develop a feeling of invincibility. All of that came to an end one moon-lit night in January 1968, the eve of the Tet Offensive. Forced to crash-land my crippled chopper under blis-tering fire from a large force of the North Vietnamese Army, I passed from a familiar realm in which I har-bored the illusion that I was in control of my destiny into a nightmare world that I could never have imag-ined.

For the next five years—three in the jungle camps of South Vietnam and two in Hanoi after a torturous six-month march along the Ho Chi Minh trail into North Vietnam—my comrades and I experienced starvation, disease, and human debasement. Of the twenty-four who were imprisoned in the jungle camps with me, nine died, and three were released by our Viet Cong captors. Only twelve of us survived to make the long journey north. We endured physical and mental torture that for some of us eventually snuffed out the will to live. Withered in body and spirit, I hovered at death's door myself, and if not for the heroic and courageous efforts of others, I would not have lived to tell of those horrible years.

Yet beyond the combat, my shoot-down, captivity, and the years of inhuman treatment as a POW, the suffering was compounded all the more by the specter of betrayal, which further dimmed the hope of sur-vival. Almost from the beginning, we prisoners found ourselves under guard by an American crossover, Marine Corps PFC Robert Garwood. His very presence disgusted and angered me because he was one of us, but the feeling that we had been betrayed was so dispiriting that it hastened the degeneration of my malnourished, disease-infested body. My mind and soul followed, though not to the end, as was the case with so many of my fellow prisoners.

Betrayal was an appropriate term to apply to Garwood because he was a weapon-bearing guard, an interpreter, an instructor in our political indoctrination, and a spy upon our actions in the jungle compounds. The same term is not so easy to apply to those bizarre occasions when my hopes of rescue, or at least those times when I sensed that fellow Americans were within striking distance of getting us out, were crushed in disappointment. Only years later, after the release of American POWs in early 1973, was I to learn just how close I had been, or should have been, to freedom. Had I known with certainty while in captivity what I discovered after coming home, I may have surrendered to despair and death as did others who gave up on life in the filth of the jungle camps.

My government knew where I was virtually the entire time I was in jungle captivity. During my debriefing after I returned to the United States, I was shown aerial photographs of the camps where I was held, and the photographs were clearly marked as having been taken during the times I was in each camp. One was taken just before an occasion in early 1971, when a helicopter combat assault stopped just short of touching down near the prison camp and staging a rescue. I looked right into the eyes of an army captain in the lead chopper that hovered forty feet over our heads, but the ships never came in. I was also shown a close-up photograph of me during my march along the Ho Chi Minh trail. My government knew where I was.

Fortunately, my nightmare came to an end. For nearly twenty-five years, however, I have agonized over other prisoners who have not come home, men who I am almost certain were in captivity and have not been accounted for. I raised that question in public speaking engagements on several occasions when I returned, and was quickly told by army officials in the Pentagon that if I wanted to continue in my army career I would cease talking about the POW issue. Nearly a quarter of a century later, the question remains unanswered and continues to leave a stain on this nation's honor because my country has failed to pursue a vigorous, uncompromising insistence that the truth be told.

I have written this book in the hope that my own experience as a prisoner of war, and afterward, can at least keep a flame flickering to light the way toward a search for the truth. This is a tale of war, yes, and I hope it offers some insights into the human struggle to prevail over horrendous, almost unimaginable suffering arising from war. But the story does not end there; it should not end there. Too many questions remain to be asked, questions that I hope will stir in the reader a demand for honest answers, and ultimately the truth.

Introduction

Through the thick afternoon air, the muted sound from a distance was distinct to my ears. The "whup-whup-whup" of helicopter blades pounded their faint, droning rhythm somewhere beyond the lush emerald jungle canopy overhead. I was the first to be conscious of the sound. I always was. The other prisoners had not yet noticed the noise as I struggled to my feet and shouted, "Choppers, guys! I hear choppers and lots of them!" The sunken eyes of the eleven frail, sickly men barely glanced toward me and then listlessly turned back to whatever they had been doing. We heard helicopters often and occasionally even saw a few flying in the distance. For three long, tortured years I had reacted the same way—always hoping, always believing that those machines would swoop down from the sky in a blaze of glory and deliver us from our living hell.

Each time something, anything, happened out of the ordinary, I hoped against hope that we were about to be set free. A lull in the artillery fire, an easing of the hateful propaganda broadcast by Hanoi Hannah, a humane gesture from one of our guards—any of these could ignite that ember of hope, if only for a moment. Any reason was good enough in my mind to justify the belief that we would finally awaken from the endless nightmare that our lives had become. On that February afternoon in 1971, I just knew it would be different.

Within a few minutes, the others had heard the blades whipping the air with that familiar "whup-whup-whup." Then, through the thick foliage that hid our camp, we saw them, flying high at about five thousand feet, fifteen of them—lines of Huey slicks and gunships, Chinooks, Cobra gunships, and OH-6 and OH-58 observation helicopters. They began spiraling downward toward us.

Our guards ran frantically toward us to herd us into the log-and-dirt-covered trench that served as a shelter against artillery and bombs. They knew that the jungle concealed us, at least for now, and did not fire at the approaching choppers so as not to reveal our exact location. As I stood at the mouthlike opening of the shelter, the other prisoners shuffled toward me as fast as their emaciated frames would allow. Six or seven guards were close at their heels. They were fully armed and wore their helmets and backpacks, obviously ready to beat a hasty retreat into the jungle if necessary.

"Di di di!," they screamed—"move!"—gesturing wildly for the prisoners to crawl into the shelter. I was shoved against the dirt wall, packed amid a knot of American and Vietnamese bodies. As the choppers drew nearer and appeared to be on the verge of land-

ing near the camp, the lead guard began to yell again: *"Di di, di di mau!"* Now they wanted us to climb out of the shelter and make our escape into the jungle, knowing that they would be trapped if the choppers inserted grounds troops to assault the camp with air support from the gunships.

As the mass of humanity began spilling out of the shelter, one of the guards was hollering, *"Mot, hi, ba. . . ."* Dammit, he was counting us! I had planned to stay put, hoping that the frightened guard would lose count or overlook me, but he poked his head into the hole and pointed his bayonet at me and ordered me out. As I emerged into the daylight, I looked up to see an observation helicopter hovering no more than forty feet above me, its skids all but touching the thatched roof of the prisoners' living hootch. Peering down on us was a black infantry captain who was perched in the open door at the rear of the chopper. He was close enough for me to see his rank and branch insignia on his camouflage uniform. He gripped a pistol in his right hand and a pair of binoculars in the other. As our eyes met, I felt the sharp sting of the bayonet in my back and heard the shrill scream of my captor: *"Di di, di di mau!"*

The whole world suddenly went into slow motion. My hundred-pound body, frail and weak from chronic dysentery and malaria, was helpless to respond to my mind's urging to turn on the guard, rip the weapon from his hands, and spring onto the roof of the hootch to my freedom aboard the helicopter. Devastated in spirit, I responded instead to the bayonet at my back and shuffled toward the jungle. I turned my face upward one last time and stared into the face of that captain. Our eyes locked for a few brief seconds, but an eternity to me. Then, as if connected by some invisible force, we shrugged our shoulders—mine in utter despair, his in complete helplessness.

Not a shot was fired. The rescue attempt was over as quickly as it had begun, and I felt my hope for life draining away with it. After the starvation, the sickness, and the misery, after we had buried almost half of our fellow prisoners, hope was losing its feeble grip.

Then, like some malevolent beast, the jungle swallowed me up once again, and the sound of freedom receded with the fading drone of those rotor blades.

1
Going to War

All day, the engine of the helicopter had been acting up, losing RPMs and causing some concern for the crew of the Huey UH-1D "slick," or transport, that was one of the most common sights during the Vietnam War. I was the copilot, or "peter pilot," during my first month of duty with the Seventy-First Assault Helicopter Company of the 145th Combat Aviation Battalion flying out of Chu Lai, in the northern highlands of what once was South Vietnam.

It was mid-May of 1967, and as a freshly minted warrant officer with only three weeks in the country, I was awed to discover how much I needed to learn about flying under *real* combat conditions. My training at Fort Wolters, Texas, and Fort Rucker, Alabama, I quickly found, just helped rookie chopper pilots get their foot in the door. The rushed but intensive two-week exposure to new maneuvers, which had been adapted to Vietnam battlefield circumstances, left me astounded with the learning curve I faced if I was to survive in the mountainous terrain of the Que Son Valley to the west. Mountain flying was even more challenging because of the higher altitudes, which reduced the available power of our already overworked delta-model Hueys.

Our unit was working in an area not far from My Lai, which was to become infamous for a controversial event there about a year later. We were making a series of practice combat assaults to drop and pick up a unit of South Vietnamese soldiers in the Army of the Republic of Vietnam, or ARVNs. The aircraft commander, or AC, had reported the engine problems earlier in the day, and the mechanics told us that when the exercise was over to bring in the ship for a check.

An Initial Shock

Then, on the third lift near a village south of Chu Lai, the motor just quit. We had been about number seven in a flight of ten ships, and from seventy feet in the air, we were forced quickly to initiate the autorotation maneuver. The ship spiraled down and crashed to the ground. For some reason, a first lieutenant who had hopped a ride to take photographs out in the boonies before going home in the next few days had decided to unbuckle his seat belt, presumably to be able to jump clear of the helicopter when it hit. Instead, the impact forced him out and up, and his body flew into the rotor blade, slicing him from his head down through his chest. He died instantly.

My greatest shock came not so much in seeing his mangled body at the crash site but later in the morgue when I was called to identify him. The flight surgeon saw my reaction and must have wondered whether that initial experience—well before I had ever gone into real combat—might psychologically damage my effectiveness. He offered to ground me, but I told him, "Hell no, I came here to fly," so he sent me back to my unit.

By all rights, finding myself twelve thousand miles from home and serving a tour of duty in Vietnam shouldn't have seemed peculiar. The early stages of the war had begun by the time I got out of high school, although the Cuban Missile Crisis had captured the public imagination far more than the obscure "police action" in remote Southeast Asia. Most people were more fearful of going to war against the Russians than were paying attention to Laos and Vietnam.

But the military had been a major influence on me all my life. Although I was born in Philadelphia and considered Philly my hometown, I was an air force brat and attended nine grade schools and four different high schools, graduating finally in 1962, in Labrador. My dad rose from an Army Air Corps enlisted man to full air force colonel in his twenty-nine-year career. He had been a radio operator and waist gunner in B-17s and B-24s during World War II. After receiving his commission, he served in the Korean War as a lieutenant.

I began college at what was then Central Missouri State at Warrensburg, after spending a couple of years working at odd jobs. While in Warrensburg, I visited a navy recruiter and asked about enlisting to become a naval aviator. He asked if my vision was twenty-twenty. I said no, and he told me that I would never be a pilot in the military, and I concluded that would be the end of my dream of flying. After finishing my freshman year, I moved back home to Newburgh,

New York, in 1965, and enrolled that fall at Orange County Community College at Middletown, New York. When I had finished my sophomore year, I learned that my Selective Service board had been looking for me, thinking that I was dodging the draft. I had begun working, first driving a beer truck, then working at a golf course, and finally taking a job at a plastics factory. I really wasn't dodging the draft, but as most normal young men at that stage in life, I was restless and confused about my direction in life.

By November 1965, my dad encouraged me to join the air force, telling me that he could arrange to get me into the missile tech school. I went to see the air force recruiter in downtown Newburgh, but a sign on the door said, "Back in twenty minutes." As I stepped back onto the sidewalk to wait for him to return, a friendly voice said, "Hello, there." It was the army recruiter from next door. "Come in and let's talk," he said, but I explained that I was waiting for the man from the air force. He was persuasive, and an hour later I had joined the army. If that weren't enough of a shock for my dad, I had joined to become a warrant officer and fly helicopters. Dad was incensed.

"Don't you know where your ass will be flying in those things?" he asked in pained exasperation. Frankly, I hadn't really thought it all through. He insisted that he would pull the necessary strings to dissolve the enlistment, or at least get it modified, but I was twenty-one, hardheaded, and too proud to turn back. I'd made my decision and stuck with it.

Within two months, I was in basic training at beautiful Fort Polk, Louisiana, and went on from there to helicopter training in Texas and Alabama. After graduating from flight school, I received my orders to report for duty on April 13, 1967, at Bien Hoa, Republic of Vietnam. The sergeant in the recruiting office had promised me that I would get to fly fixed-wing airplanes, which eventually came true. It just took the army seventeen years and no small amount of aggravation, grief, and pain to me, before it kept that promise.

Life Was Good

I had first reported to the Seventy-First in April, shortly after I arrived at Bien Hoa near Saigon. The company was within two weeks of moving north to Chu Lai on the coast of the South China Sea, and the two weeks awaiting the move were like a real holiday. We had a comfortable compound with plenty of good food, a bar, and American nurses who lived in a villa just across the street. Life in the Honour-Smith compound was good, very good, but all good things must come to an end. When the order came down, we flew the company en masse up to our new position with the headquarters on the beach, and I began to prepare for taking my place in the war.

The company was composed of three platoons, two of which performed transport missions and were designated by the radio call sign "Rattler." The gunship platoon was designated "Firebird." I joined the second platoon as a peter pilot with the "slicks," the UH-1 Hueys that transported troops and supplies on what we called "ash and trash" missions. Of course, such relatively routine missions were possible only after a unit of troops had taken control of a field position. Getting a unit into the position in the first place required a combat assault, in which the slicks would be escorted by as many as six gunships. That initial drop-off of troops and supplies, or "insertion," could get perilously exciting if the enemy wanted to prevent our troops from occupying the landing zone.

My introduction to the heavily armed charlie-model gunships would not come for a few months, but I was able to acquire a reputation very quickly with the slicks as a "magnet ass" for my ability to attract trouble, often in the form of bullets. In June, a mission took us into the Que Son Valley where we were hit by an air burst from an North Vietnamese Army, or NVA, antiaircraft gun that put a fist-sized hole in our rotor blade. The whole ship began to vibrate severely. The aircraft commander managed to maneuver the crippled ship toward a unit of American troops near the village of Tien Phuoc, where we put down and waited for the maintenance officer to arrive. He covered the damage with 100-mph tape—a high-tech version of duct tape—and flew us back to Chu Lai to get another slick.

Within an hour after we returned to the area, we took heavy small arms fire, with one round hitting the turbine and the compressor area that forced us to set the chopper down in a field and wait once again for the "snake doctor" to return to do his magic on the craft. We said something about heading back to get another one, and the exasperated officer looked at us and said, "Like hell! I don't have enough ships for you to keep bringing out here and getting shot up!" We were through for the day and got an early start back at the bar.

Those two shoot-downs were my closest encounters with the enemy in the early going. Most of our missions, although we flew for ten to twelve hours a day as opposed to four or five for the gunships, passed without very much drama. Mostly we ran routine "ash and trash" calls, although the deeper we got into 1967, the more intense life became. In early July, we got a medivac call—medical evacuation—to extract wounded. Even though we had cover from the gunships, we were taking heavy enemy small arms fire from the bush. We set the chopper down, and an American soldier came running from the tree line holding his German shepherd scout dog that had been shot. He was upset and in tears as he tenderly placed the bleeding dog in the back of the chopper, and all I could think of was, "We're getting our asses shot at and this guy's worried about a dog?" We pulled away with bullets spitting past us and returned to the field hospital. At least the dog was still alive when we dropped him off.

Bloody Body Bags

A few weeks later, I was flying as peter pilot—the position I kept as long as I was flying slicks—with Mike Sweeney, who was the coolest pilot under fire I'd seen to that point. We had arrived at a just-occupied U.S. fire base to pick up wounded. Sweeney had spiraled the chopper down tightly and quickly to minimize our exposure to possible ground fire. He did not set the chopper down on the pad but hovered lightly with the skids just inches above the ground, thus saving precious seconds when we took off again. Several GIs rushed up and threw five big, blood-smeared body bags into the back, and I assumed they were Americans. That was my first sight of bloody body bags, and Sweeney must have noticed the look in my eye. Then all at once a sniper began shooting at us from the perimeter of the fire base. Sweeney coolly said, "You fly us out of here." I guess he wanted to force me out of my fixation on the body bags and to concentrate my mind and reflexes instead on the necessity of saving the ship and our butts.

One of my last slick missions sent us in mid-July to insert a six-member, long-range reconnaissance patrol—LRRP—into a tiny landing zone in a densely forested hillside. We were to perform two fake landings besides the actual drop-off, which was the second approach. The false landings were designed to confuse the enemy as to where we actually inserted the troops. We circled for awhile to make sure that all was well when within two or three minutes the LRRP commander whispered excitedly into the radio, "Come back and get us, Rattler, they're all over us!"

When we went back in to get them, the crew chief and the door gunner were hyped with adrenaline. Huge trees reached up fifty feet to our left and right. As we touched down, the patrol came running out of the tree line. No more than seven to ten seconds passed before we lifted off, and at least fifty small arms opened up in a blistering field of fire while our door gunners blasted back. We were hit by several bullets, and the covering gunships each took two rounds.

That mission caused a great change to come over me. I went from being new, puckered, and scared to being angry. I had seen too often that we were putting too many guys on a hilltop only to return two weeks later to take them off, and then put them back again at the same hilltop a few weeks later. I began to ask myself: What kind of war is this? That was the moment that the anger forced from me the question: What do I have to do so that I can shoot back?

2
Shooting Back

In Vietnam there were no battle lines. You were as likely to take enemy fire in a placid village as you were from a dense tree line at the edge of a rice paddy—or anywhere while cruising at treetop level during a routine resupply mission. For three months I had been on the receiving end of that fire, twice getting knocked out of the sky. I wanted to start shooting back, and that couldn't happen while I was flying the slicks.

After the last LRRP operation, I had asked about going to the guns, but the other pilots said that I hadn't been there long enough. The gunship pilots needed at least four months of flying or at least two hundred hours in the slicks. But one day in late July of 1967, a gun pilot came running into the hootch and said, "We need a pilot!" Since I was all alone in the room, he didn't have any choice. I jumped into the jeep that carried us to the flight line to the waiting "hog," a UH-1C Huey armed with two pods each of twenty-four rockets and two M-60 machine guns pointing from the open door on each side of the aircraft. As peter pilot on this virgin flight with the guns, my job basically was to fly along and watch.

"Farmers" Shoot Back

We were called farther out west into the Que Son Valley than I had ever been. A LRRP team observing a wide, flat area had called in a fire mission against what they said was a group of thirty enemy soldiers. When we came in, all we could see were about thirty farmers working in the field. We called back and asked for clarification, and the LRRPs verified that they were Viet Cong tending their fields. I was concerned that we might be attacking civilians, but we rolled in and started shooting. The "farmers" threw down their tools, picked up their rifles and started shooting back. Our door gunner, Charles Sanders, was hit in the mouth by a ricocheting bullet and blood was everywhere. It turned out to look worse than it was, but that was the first person that I'd seen get shot. By the time our gunships had finished their runs, we had taken out twenty of the enemy soldiers and headed back to Chu Lai. I was invited soon after to move my gear into the gun hootch and became a gunship peter pilot with the Firebirds, the platoon distinguished by the menacing scarlet war bird painted on the side of the chopper.

After moving from the second platoon hootch into the Firebird quarters, I felt strange and a little awed, almost as if I didn't deserve to be there. As a slick pilot, I invariably spent more than my fair share of time in the officers club. We had it built right on the

beach in Chu Lai, a simple thatched hut in the sand.
Every day after the sun went down, if we weren't
flying, most of us would be hoisting drinks at the
club.

We bought books of tickets from the club officers,
with each book containing forty tickets worth a quarter each, the price of a drink. As a troopship pilot, I
had normally drunk up four full books of tickets each
month. As a gunship pilot, I would find myself in-
vesting in six or seven books a month. In a way, the
period spent between missions was almost surreal and
at times almost bizarre.

Many of the men in our unit, as with GIs throughout Vietnam, were not even old enough to drink in
their home states. They sought ways to fill their idle
time to limit thinking about the war beyond the security of the rear area. For many, drinking filled that
time. They had been sent thousands of miles to fight
an enemy who hid in the jungle and rarely appeared
in full view to engage in that fight, and yet the war,
like some odd sort of football game, would be interrupted by time-outs. Those we were supposed to kill
were not easily distinguished from those who were
our allies, and even they changed sides like the wind.

Helicopter crews were a curiosity in their own
right. Up front were two young, almost grown men.
In the back were usually a couple of kids—eighteen-
year-old, machine gun-toting kids. Now and then, one
of the two might be a seasoned veteran—a twenty-
one-year-old serving his second tour. The door gunners sat sidesaddle halfway toward the rear of the
ship. Each had his own little cubbyhole amid ammo
cans and smoke grenades, while the rotor blades
whipped and roared above his head. Below was the

war, that tragicomedy of errors, and it was often a maddening, perplexing affair.

Now that I had become a gunship pilot, things would change even more for me. That first mission had just taken me along for the ride, but now I would get to participate in the running gunfights with a wily, elusive enemy. I learned to handle the fear of being shot at while shooting back at the same time. I also worked my way up quickly to six or more little ticket books each month.

With the Firebirds, the missions were shorter but often under heavy fire. What the gunships gave away in time per mission with a lower fuel load, they made up for in the firepower of their armaments. I became a wingman who covered the lead chopper, which was usually a hog. Besides the two M-60 machine guns and two seven-shot rocket pods, my ship was mounted on each side with a minigun, similar to a Gatling gun, that was usually operated by the peter pilot and could fire up to six thousand rounds of ammunition per minute. This was my weapon of choice, and I missed firing it after I became an aircraft commander by the end of August 1967. After being the target of so many Viet Cong bullets without the ability to shoot back, I now felt like a gunfighter in the old West. Sure, I was getting shot at, but now I was shooting back with far more firepower than I was receiving. Nothing brings a man into more fearsomely intimate contact with reality than to be shot at, but I discovered an exhilarating feeling of power with that minigun at my command. I had grown to feel invincible, as if it were impossible to shoot me. Maybe it was a necessary psychological survival mechanism, but it took such a mental state to regulate the balance between paralyzing fear and a consuming, war-crazed sense of hatred directed at a usually invisible enemy who was trying every way possible to kill me.

No-Shoot Orders

These raging emotions created an aggressiveness in gunship crews, almost a devil-may-care intensity. I was not immune to the transforming effect of the war. During a three-day truce agreed to by the U.S. command in September to recognize Vietnamese Independence Day, I was flying in a formation south of Chu Lai along Highway One with a new platoon leader who was timid about flying whenever the bullets were. Flying under no-shoot orders, we passed over three fully uniformed NVA soldiers carrying AK-47 assault rifles and wearing pith helmets. As we flew over, one of them gave us the finger. I called the platoon leader and said, "Did you see those three NVA?" He said, "Yeah, Nine-Zero, I saw them." I radioed back, "I'm gonna shoot 'em." He replied, "Negative, follow me back to Chu Lai. You can't shoot them, there's a cease-fire."

At first, I thought OK, but after a half mile I said to myself, "Bullshit, this is a goddamn war." Unnoticed by the platoon leader, I wheeled around, swept into position, and blew away the NVA soldiers with the minigun and hurried back to rejoin the formation. When we landed, I told the crew chief and gunner quietly and casually to rearm the minigun because I'd fired about two hundred rounds. Unfortunately, the platoon leader saw the men reloading and confronted me. He told me that I could be court-martialed for violating a cease-fire, but in this absurd war of even more absurd "rules," nothing else was ever said about the incident.

In early November, while on a mission out in the Que Son area, we got a call from a command and control (C&C) ship to look along a ridgeline to the west for a group of twenty woodcutters. We approached the area and saw the men on the hillside. They were dressed in black pajamas and had bundles of wood strapped on their backs—labor usually reserved for women and children. We flew over them and waved, and they waved back. Then the command and control ship said, "Nine-Zero, put some rounds with the minigun out in front of them and make them turn around." I went down, shot the first six or seven of them, and they fell, wounded or dead. The colonel in the C&C ship went crazy. "Firebird, I told you, goddammit, to fire out in front of them!" I casually responded, "Well, it's out in front of the rest of them."

After the bodies had been searched, my instincts were justified. They were not just woodcutters but Viet Cong woodcutters. The rest of them got away.

Such instances only reinforced my growing sense of frustration with the war. More and more, I began asking myself what the hell we were doing there anyway. I decided that I wanted out, that the war was a waste of time, not to mention good men. I wanted to serve out my tour and somehow find a way to avoid a second. The Vietnamese we were helping were worthless as soldiers. My disillusionment was growing almost with each passing day as I realized that the war was deteriorating into a high-energy blunder factory and that we would never be allowed to win it.

A Weird War Indeed

Yet this weird war always found a way to become even more weird. By December 1967, the shooting virtually stopped. I don't think I fired a round the whole month before I left on December 28 to try to find some sanity during R&R in Bangkok. The week there was restful, expensive, and pleasant, and I was able to leave the war behind temporarily. But the weirdness managed to catch up with me on my last day in Bangkok before returning to Vietnam.

I visited a Buddhist monastery which was the site of the "Sleeping Buddha," an impressive, eighty-foot statue of the reclining Buddha. I wandered through the shrine for a short time and then dropped some change from my pocket into the collection box as I left. One of the saffron-robed monks quickly approached me. He was a short man, about forty, with very short black hair. He placed his hand on my shoulder and thanked me profusely for my donation, which I found a little embarrassing. Then he asked if I would like a tour of the rest of the monastery, which I accepted. I thanked him when we returned to the gate, but he refused to let me leave just yet. He reached around his neck and removed a necklace made of woven orange string that bore a thin silver medallion, about one-inch square, with an image of Buddha etched into its surface. He lifted the necklace over my head and gently placed it around my neck. His black eyes peered deeply into mine, and he told me, "As long as you never take this medal off, you will always be safe."

The next day, I returned to Vietnam to resume the

unfinished business of war as usual. Back in Chu Lai that afternoon, as I climbed into my flight suit, I nonchalantly removed the medallion and dropped it into my footlocker. Within thirty-six hours, I would have reason to wonder for the rest of my life—even to this day—whether the monk knew something that I should have heeded. If so, I didn't honor his simple act of generosity, and I will never know for sure whether he could have intervened in my destiny, because the medallion vanished, as I was about to for five long, agonizing years.

3
Shoot-down

On January 4, 1968, I returned to Da Nang from Bangkok and was told that I would have to wait my turn for at least five days before I could catch a flight down to Chu Lai. That suited me fine because I wanted to go to Anh Khe to visit some buddies in the First Cavalry. While I was standing there, though, I met one of the slick pilots from the Seventy-First who was just leaving for his R&R, and he told me that all hell had broken loose in Chu Lai. A couple of ships had been shot down, and Mark Leopold, one of our pilots, had been wounded. I decided on the spot to go back immediately. I went to an army enlisted man who was standing in line to board a P-3 Orion and offered him fifty dollars and my numbered chit, which gave him an extra five-day layover before returning to the field, in exchange for his chit. Two hours later, I was standing on the flight line at Chu Lai.

By the time I reached my company area, the flight schedule for the next day's crews had already been posted, but I had no trouble at the bar talking one of the Firebird aircraft commanders into letting me fly in his place the next day. Frank Carson was to be my peter pilot. Carson was being groomed to become an AC, and he was required to fly with each of the "old hand" pilots in the platoon before he could qualify. I was the last one scheduled to supervise Carson, so I would turn over the controls to him for any missions we were called on that day.

Answering the Call

Because of the increased enemy activity, we decided to move our choppers to Hill Thirty-Five on the outskirts of Chu Lai so that we could move to the action faster—in ten to twelve minutes rather than fifteen to twenty. We got settled in by midmorning and waited. The first call came about noon while we were eating a lunch of C-rations. I gave Carson the pilot's seat and climbed into the other side to man the minigun. Our formation headed east from Highway One across the flat, tree-dotted, sandy terrain toward the South China Sea. The Americal Division unit that had called for us had four to six VC on the run, and our job was to try to cut them off. After spotting their position and identifying the VC the grunts were chasing, we rolled in and blasted them in short order, then returned to Hill Thirty-Five to refuel and rearm.

At two o'clock we got another call, back into the same area to escort a combat assault of five troopships that was to reinforce the unit where the skirmish had taken place earlier that afternoon, although we encountered no hostile action. A third run at five o'clock was equally uneventful, so we returned to refuel, re-arm, and eat supper.

I had finished eating about six o'clock and sat down to write a letter to a high school classmate, Barbara Martin. I wrote that I was "short"—with only a couple of months left in my tour of duty, and hoped that we would not be called out any more that day because I hated to fly at night in Vietnam.

In the daylight, we could fly much lower, usually right down on the treetops. The VC had a hard time hitting us when we were that low because they saw us for only a brief second or two. At night, however, we couldn't see well enough to get safely down on the deck. My writing was interrupted by the call to scramble, and I had to put the letter aside and hurry out to the ship. It was about seven o'clock and was just about to turn dark. The letter lay on the table, unfinished. I learned years later that someone had picked it up, sealed it, and mailed it. Twenty-five or so years later, she told me personally that she had indeed received the letter.

Within three minutes, our gunships were in the air and heading west toward Charlie Company, Third of the Twenty-First, of the 196th Light Infantry Brigade, which was being pounded deep within the Que Son Valley in a three-pronged ambush by a large element of what we had assumed to be Viet Cong. I had taken command of the ship because Carson really wasn't ready for this kind of baptism by fire, and I just had a premonition about this particular mission.

Charlie Company had formed a night perimeter and settled in to eat supper and open some mail and belated Christmas packages that had been choppered in earlier in the day. Then, just after dark, the gates of hell flew open. More than eighty Americans were killed or wounded within the first few minutes of the firefight, and the position was almost instantly over-run by an overwhelming enemy force. As we dialed into the unit's radio frequency, we knew immediately the gravity of the situation. The Viet Cong had not ambushed Charlie Company. The heavy assault was the work of the crack Second NVA Division.

We didn't know it at the time, but the bloodiest period of the entire Vietnam War was about to begin. This slaughter in the Que Son Valley, and others like it to follow, was among the first battles in the massive effort that history now recognizes as the 1968 Tet Offensive.

Our radio blared with pleas for help. The voices from Goblin Three-One were frantic and desperate. Under withering machine-gun and mortar fire, the grunts had almost exhausted their ammunition and were calling for artillery to be laid down virtually on their own position. As we approached, shells already were pounding the jungle in and around the battle scene. Our choppers were directed to orbit a couple of miles north and await the end of the barrage. By the time we were able to return, we had begun to run low on fuel. Factoring in the travel time to and from Hill Thirty-Five and our orbiting, we had only about ten minutes remaining of actual "on-station" time, and time for those GIs was running out.

We proceeded toward the firefight and called the troops on the ground: "Goblin Three-One, this is Fire-bird. How can we assist you?" A frightened voice called out for some rockets on both sides of their po-sition. In the darkness, though, we saw their position was impossible and that we were in danger of hitting our own troops with rocket and machine-gun fire. Gary McCall, the AC of the lead gunship, called for the troops to pop a couple of flares, then he rolled in at a hundred knots to place eight rockets to the left of the easternmost flare. McCall turned to the right and drew a stream of tracer rounds toward his chopper from below.

As wingman, I normally covered his break by pouring rockets and a barrage of fire from the minigun and the M-60s in hopes that the enemy would duck and allow the attacking ship to evade the counterfire. This, however, was not the usual burst of sporadic small-arms bullets we had become accustomed to. The jungle beneath the lead chopper lit up like the Fourth of July, the light coming from rifles, but mostly from fifty-caliber guns spewing huge red-orange tracer rounds.

"Taking Hits, Taking Hits"

With that arsenal down there, I became a sitting duck. Instinctively, I flipped off my running and strobe lights, but it was too late. Dozens of blazing tracers whizzed by the nose of my chopper. Next, I felt a couple of slight lurches and heard the dull "thruck-thruck" of rounds whacking somewhere back near the tail boom. I radioed right away, "Nine-Zero is taking hits, taking hits!" I climbed up and away, but the chopper was hit several more times. "Nine-Four, Nine-Zero has been shot up pretty good," I called to McCall over my radio.

Just after I indicated that we ought to return to Chu Lai, I saw McCall turning and nosing down to make another run at the NVA positions. Reflex overpowered my reason and fear, so I swept around to provide more covering fire for his attack. I could see from the spray of tracers, which were only every sixth or seventh round in an ammunition belt, that the lead ship was taking many hits. As I descended to cover his break, the gunfire quickly turned on me. I heard more bullets smashing into my chopper, then the smell of burning hydraulic fluid began to pervade the cockpit. Seconds later, the lights on my dash console began a dancing light show. First, yellow lights flickered. Then the red ones joined in and began to flash, but the deadly light show outside our crippled aircraft also demanded my attention. To make matters worse, I could feel a definite stiffening within the flight controls.

Suddenly, at an altitude of four hundred feet and a speed of a hundred knots, the chopper began to surge and lurch, resisting my efforts to stabilize its line of flight. The severity of the malfunction demanded every ounce of brute strength I could summon through a series of frantic yanks and jerking shoves just to keep us in the air.

I radioed that I was heading for Chu Lai. Ahead of us loomed a large hill that under normal circumstances would require a simple maneuver to climb up and over the additional three hundred feet in elevation. But the hydraulic damage was too severe, and I knew we were in trouble. I pulled on the collective pitch lever with my left hand to start a climb to take us over the approaching hillside. *Dammit!* There was absolutely no movement, no climb. Instead, the aircraft began the first of several repetitions of a nasty maneuver that I had never experienced. The nose dropped instantly and severely, while at the same time the craft began a violent roll to the left. I yanked harder on the collective, as I simultaneously applied all the pressure back and to the right that I could force to the cyclic control in my right hand. The helicopter immediately displayed all the flight characteristics of a rock.

Although we had managed to limp out of the line of lethal ground fire above the battlefield, I quickly sensed that I no longer had full control of the aircraft. I yelled for Carson to get on the controls with me so that maybe between the two of us we could muscle the chopper toward home. Our efforts, while partially successful, also shifted our crippled craft into a slow right turn—heading us back in the direction where our troubles had started in the first place. At least the change in direction took us out of the collision course with the hill we had been fast approaching. In the ensuing minutes, we fought a constant battle for control of the aircraft and struggled to prevent the possibility of the chopper rolling completely upside down. Each time, Carson and I had managed to right ourselves, but the ship was frozen in the direction we were heading. Both of us realized that we were not going to fly that machine out of that valley that night. We had enough fuel and just enough control to land it, but only if we hurried.

The Fear Factor

I radioed the grunts several times and asked them to provide a signal toward which I could crash-land. I thought that with the four of us and our weapons we could be of some help to them on the ground, plus by being together there could be a more centralized rescue effort. But I failed to take into account the fear factor. Those grunts were isolated and surrounded and probably close to a state of shock. They didn't want to illuminate their position for fear the enemy could pinpoint them. For the next several minutes, I alternated between begging and pleading for help, but to no avail.

Over and over, the grunt on the other end of the radio calls came back with the same frightened reply, "Wait one!" For eight and a half minutes he answered my begging with the same repetition of those two words, "Wait one!" He was so stricken with fear that he could not think clearly, could not recognize that we could have helped each other. He was afraid to give away his location, but his panic was blocking the obvious from his mind—he had already been overrun, and the enemy already knew his position.

Now my only hope was to get the ship on the ground with as little injury to my crew as possible. The flight controls were frozen in position, so I was reduced to manipulating the throttle to ease the descent. We had dropped from four hundred feet to just about treetop level and began to draw gunfire again. I was looking desperately for an open area to put down when suddenly, at a height of about fifty feet, the trees melted away to reveal a huge rice paddy. Unfortunately, the dikes ran perpendicular to our line of flight. Had they been parallel, we could have landed between them, but now we couldn't avoid them. At thirty feet, I rolled off the throttle and then shut off the engine to lessen the likelihood of an explosion or fire if the fuel tank ruptured. Suddenly, it got very quiet, almost dead silent, as the engine wound down. We dropped hard and fast toward the ground, skimming one dike, but the next one appeared right in front of us. I hauled back with both hands on the cyclic, raising the nose of the craft just enough to slow our forward speed a little before we hit.

Then came the impact, a very hard jolt. We bounced back into the air, punched the ground again and skidded along the muddy earth. As we slid to a stop, the ship turned a little and caused a roll to the left. We tipped over on our side. Both rotor blades disintegrated as they slammed into the heavy, muddy soil and the huge dike. The remains of the doomed gunship came to rest on its left side.

Out of the Wreckage

Probably no more than a few seconds passed, although it seemed much longer. The crew and I lay still, then as if in a coordinated single movement we all bolted for the only exit, the open right door that pointed skyward, and each of us in turn climbed up and out of the wreckage. Once free of the aircraft, we found ourselves ankle-deep in mud with bullets whizzing past us from the tree lines that surrounded us. Robert Lewis, my crew chief, and Jim Pfister, the doorgunner, headed west from the nose section. Carson and I slipped toward the north, making our way as fast as we could in the muck, alternating between a crouching run and a lowcrawl. We climbed over two of the five-foot dikes and scrambled over a third before we stopped to catch our breath and collect our wits about us.

In the light of the nearly full moon I could see McCall's gunship moving low and fast trying to come in to get us. I figured that the crew probably could

see the wreckage, but there was no way they could
see us. Then McCall began taking heavy gunfire, so
he flew up and away. At first, I was worried about
him, worried that he would end up in there with us,
and I was relieved that he got away. Years later, Spec.
Five Ray Foley, McCall's crew chief, would tell me
that he extended his tours twice because he said that
he didn't want to go home until the other crew made
it out. He felt as if he were leaving us. If only others
later had been so dedicated to our rescue as he had
been.

Only after I saw the gunship fly safely away did I
realize that we had been left terribly alone. As I lay
in the mud amid the mayhem of that night, I sensed
for the first time that awful, empty feeling. Unfortunately, it would not be the last time that feeling would
pervade my body and soul.

While the bullets were zinging overhead as we
huddled behind the dike, Carson insisted that we had
to get out of there. I said, "We need to stay here. This
is where they're going to come to get us. This has
happened to me twice before, and they've always gotten me out." He looked at the gun flashes from less
than fifty yards away in the tree line and whispered
earnestly, "No way anybody's going to get in here."
He was right. My previous shoot-downs had never
been like that night. I wasn't thinking rationally because if I had been, I would know that whoever shot
me down would never allow anybody to get in there
and get us out. No helicopter had been built that could
survive the volume of fire that had been hurled at us
that night.

Carson insisted he was getting out of that area. I
pointed toward the river, which was more than two

hundred yards on the other side of where our chopper had crashed. That was his only way out. "You do what you think is right," I told him, "but I'm staying here." He scampered off, zigzagging to avoid the hail of bullets being fired at him. From my right, I could see a shadowy horde of NVA, yelling and shooting in pursuit across the rice paddy, trying to intercept Carson before he reached the other side and the shelter of the trees as well as the transporting flow of the small river. I thought he was dead for sure, but I learned years later that he got away. He had evaded enemy soldiers for two full days and nights, finally making his way to freedom.

That Lonely Feeling

Now I really was alone. For the rest of the night, I lay against the dike trying to gouge out a notch in the base large enough to crawl into. If I could just dig in, I knew that I would be relatively safe from both the friendly artillery fire and the enemy soldiers who were trying to locate me. But the muck was so soft that it kept collapsing as I scooped frantically at the wall of the dike. Even so, I knew that the choppers would be coming at first light in the morning to rescue me. I just needed to stay hidden until sunrise.

For the rest of the night, I would doze off for a few minutes at a time. I could not believe how bright it seemed to be, but the adrenaline must have sharpened my sense of sight. Several times I watched the NVA moving back and forth at about one-hour intervals toward the crash site to strip it of weapons and ammunition, intervals that coincided with the end of American artillery air bursts that sprayed the area from one hundred feet high with shrapnel. Shards of deadly metal were slamming and pinging off the wreckage of my chopper. The NVA troops would take cover just before the next series of rounds was fired as if they were listening in to the American communications at the fire direction center. That fierce incoming artillery was another reason why I wanted to dig into the base of the dike.

Within an hour or so of dawn, one of the most bizarre things I have ever experienced occurred. I was stirred from a light sleep by what I thought was the sound of a helicopter. That was odd because I noticed when I awoke that a dense fog had covered the area about fifteen feet above the ground. Flying a helicopter through that fog would have required some method or device to coordinate the flight instruments and keep the craft in an even, steady hover. Controlling the Hueys we flew at that time in a level path would have been impossible to sustain under those conditions of zero visibility. Yet I looked directly above me and saw a white chopper. It hovered for twenty to thirty seconds and then disappeared. If it had been a little to the left or right, the crew would have seen me, but they didn't. No shots were fired from the tree line. It was as if a ghost had appeared for a brief moment and then vanished into thin air.

Mysterious Capabilities

People since then have said that I was either dreaming or hallucinating, but I am absolutely certain of what I saw. A high-ranking officer, after I revealed the mysterious experience, told me years later that the United States had aircraft during the war with secret capabilities and that "they" had sophisticated equipment that we mere combat pilots didn't have. In Da Nang on several occasions I had seen CIA aircraft just like the one I saw in that fog, and I can only guess at who "they" were hovering over that muddy rice paddy so many years ago.

For the next hour I watched the morning begin to break. When I saw how thick the fog was, my heart sank. I must have dozed off again, but at seven o'clock or so I woke up to see an enemy soldier standing directly above me, but he didn't see me. He walked a few feet along the top of the dike, turned around and walked past me again, but at the last second he spotted me, excitedly turned his AK-47 rifle on me, and motioned for me to get up. I tried, but the crash had hurt my back and knees, and spending the night in the mud had left me even stiffer. I tried to stand but slid back down, then struggled to get to my feet. Any thought of trying to resist evaporated when I caught sight of three other NVA soldiers within twenty feet. I finally managed to stand and put my hands above my head. My captor handed me a card printed in English: "You are a prisoner of the People's National Liberation Front. You will not be harmed. You will be humanely treated. If you show progress, you may be released."

I read the card, but its full meaning did not sink in. They were English words, but my mind had gone numb. Through the fog I could hear choppers in the distance not far away, but that distance was now like a million miles away.

4
Into the Jungle

In the distance, I could hear the helicopters waiting for the fog to lift before moving in to search for the men left behind from the action the night before. My captors led me toward the downed aircraft. We passed my flight helmet that I must have thrown down during our rush across the rice paddy, and I assumed that the helmet had given a clue as to which way we had gone in trying to escape. We reached the wreckage and then turned along the direction that Lewis and Pfister had taken toward the tree line.

When we arrived at the edge of the rice paddy, a trail led into the woods and past a bamboo and grass hootch. It was invisible from the rice paddy and came into view only from a close distance. Inside, some women and a few soldiers sat around a small fire, laughing, gesturing at me, and making comments in Vietnamese. As I was led along the trail deeper into the woods, I noticed a lot of commo wire running in all directions along the ground. No doubt, the NVA had an extensive communications system, one that probably was listening in and relaying the messages of the American artillery and other combat units. But no more than five minutes after I had been moved out of the rice paddy, U.S. artillery opened up again, and the guards started pushing me into a dead run. As the rounds began to land nearer, the guards jumped into a hole at the front of a big mound. I just stood there, laughing at them and saying, "It won't hurt you!" Fortunately, none of the rounds came close enough to do any damage. On reflection, I must have been in shock to be so irrational, so unbelievably dumb.

After the incoming rounds had ceased, the NVA crawled out of the shelter and moved me down the trail. Every few minutes, they would slow down and make a little whistling sound, which was followed by another whistle from sentries concealed somewhere in the bush. They ran and walked me in a northwesterly direction for about twenty minutes before we came around a sharp bend in the trail to a huge boulder the size of a car. They sat me down, and within a few minutes Lewis and Pfister appeared. A few guards brought them into the clearing from the same direction that I had come.

Now There Were Three

I learned from them days later that during their escape from the wreckage, they hid near the tree line that was right at the point where the trail led into the thick of the NVA troops that sprung the ambush against Charlie Company and knocked down our chopper. At nearly dawn, because it was still almost dark, the NVA spotted Pfister's white face but had not detected

Lewis, who was black. When Pfister was captured, he stood up, looked at Lewis, and said, "Lew, they got us." His hiding place exposed, Lewis retorted, "Pfister, if we ever get out of this alive, I'll kill you." They would get out alive, all right, but not for more than five long years.

Lewis had not been my crew chief for long, but he had performed courageously throughout the firefight that eventually brought down our chopper. He had sustained a back injury similar to mine and was plagued by it for the duration of our captivity. One of the strengths of Lewis's character was his determination. Even though he fell ill with malaria almost as soon as we were captured and suffered terribly from that and other diseases in the years to follow, his determination helped to sustain others even as he struggled to survive.

Pfister, my door gunner, who hailed from Indiana, was well liked for his sense of humor. The previous night's mission had been the first that we had flown together. Small in stature, he had a huge heart and a ready smile, and although his health seriously failed in the months to come, he did all in his power to help those who were worse off than he was. A natural-born con artist, he was to teach us all a thing or two about finagling tobacco, candy, and other meager concessions from the Vietnamese because he made it his business to learn their language, especially their swear words.

While the three of us were standing by the rock, a leader who looked to be half Vietnamese and half Caucasian appeared. He spoke excellent English, and we dubbed him "Frenchie," thinking that he might have been part French, born of a father who had

served in the colonial war. Frenchie began to inter-
rogate us. He asked me my unit, and I lied, telling
him that I had been flying a medivac ship. He said,
"You're a liar. I'll tell you your unit. You're with the
Seventy-First, Firebirds, supporting the 196th." Then
he pulled out a map case and produced a detailed map
of the entire Que Son Valley. He noted the positions
of different American units and various fire bases,
pinpointing LZ Ross in particular. He explained the
tactics of the three-pronged ambush that had chewed
up Charlie Company the night before. He pointed out
the location and plan for a similar attack that would
target Delta Company next—and it did, that night,
with equally disastrous results for the Americans, as
we would learn in a matter of days.

After delivering a harsh speech about the importance of our cooperating, emphasizing that they knew
everything anyway, Frenchie disappeared. Our guards
began walking us again toward what I thought was
the northwest, almost a forced march for two hours.
They stopped us abruptly and demanded that we remove our boots. I protested loudly and argued with
the one who seemed to be in charge. Why I was persuasive I don't know, but for some reason I still don't
understand, he relented. My sharp tongue and belligerent attitude expressed that afternoon for the first
time quickly became characteristic for me in respond-
ing to my captors, a personality trait that hardly en-
deared me to them.

Shortly after my trailside protest, we continued until we reached a well-concealed place under the triple
canopy forest to stop for lunch. They gave us rice
balls to eat, which began a prolonged fast on my part
because I had hated rice even at home and refused to

eat it. I went without food other than an occasional banana for fifteen days—not necessarily a smart thing to do.

For two weeks, the Vietnamese walked us around in circles, although we generally were moving west. We crossed a wide valley somewhere in the distant reaches of the Que Son Valley and started making our way toward the mountains on the other side. After a week, we came to an old house where we stayed the night in a bomb shelter with its entrance hidden under the bed of the old woman who lived there. She appeared to be about ninety and had a kindly face. When we arrived, she looked at my feet and pointed at them. I gathered that she was gesturing toward my socks and asking me to remove them. They were filthy and wet from a week's march, so I took them off, wrung them out, and handed them to her. She handed me a clean white pair. The next morning, she returned my socks clean and dry. Such acts of charity, I was to learn soon, would be painfully rare in my life for a long time to come.

A Glimpse of the Enemy

The next day, we stopped at a temporary camp where we were offered a small portion of meat in our rice, but I still refused to eat. I had yet to realize that my self-imposed fast was of little consequence to my Vietnamese captors and very soon would hasten my vulnerability to several physical afflictions that would almost cost me my life. But in the short stay at this camp, I saw a glimpse of the human side of the adversary we were up against. About 150 battle-weary NVA soldiers, some of them wounded, came into the area and handed over their rifles to another group of fresh troops just waiting to slink eastward into the jungle where they would carry on the war against the men we'd been separated from, some of whom eventually would join us.

We kept moving southwest toward the mountains, which were so steep that wood-reinforced steps had been cut into the trail. I was becoming weaker with each passing day, and Pfister didn't help matters with his constant, repetitive singing of a popular song of about that time, "Give Me a Ticket for an Airplane." I still was not eating, and my back and knees that had been banged up from the crash were making each step a painful ordeal. Also, fear was finally beginning to settle in. No one with us spoke English, so I also felt increasingly isolated, although we three prisoners managed to communicate on a limited basis during the days we were on the march.

After we had crossed the mountains, we trudged down into a little valley where there was a large bamboo and thatch complex of many rooms set out in a rice paddy. My hunger was becoming ravenous now. Besides the few bananas I was able to eat, I contented myself by filling my belly with water from the streams, which was unwise and an invitation to disease. This also sent the guards into fits of rage because we were not drinking the boiled water in the canteens they carried. At this latest camp, the others tried to get me to eat. The guards had put out a cooked chicken, which helped some, but when that was gone, I realized that I was going to have to overcome my objections to rice if I was going to survive.

These few days at this site were uneventful and almost casual. We began to talk of escape, thinking that if the security was no tighter than we had seen recently, we could gain a four-or five-hour head start before we were missed. Then, as if on cue, several armed guards stepped around the corner. There was no way that they could have heard us or even understood what we were saying, but Frenchie's words came back like a slap across the face: "We know everything anyway." End of escape plan.

On the third day in that camp, Frenchie reappeared and began interrogating us. I gave him my name, rank, and serial number. Then he produced a U.S. issue forty-five caliber pistol in a dark brown leather pistol belt with "U.S." tooled into the surface. "If you don't answer my questions, I'm going to kill you right here, right now," he said to me. I looked him in the eye and asked, "Can I say one thing?" He said yes. Then I explained: "I'm a helicopter pilot, a warrant officer, and that's all I know. I don't know strategy. I don't know anything about the 196th. All I know is that helicopter." He smiled and said, "OK." Then he separately interrogated Lewis and Pfister. No one was shot.

After a few more days at the camp, a guard came to us and said, "No talk." Just behind him came four other Americans: Richard Williams, David Harker, Jim Strickland, and Francis Cannon. They were members of Delta Company who had been captured after the three-pronged ambush explained to us by Frenchie the morning of our capture.

In the third week of January 1968, the seven of us prisoners were marched at a steady pace along an erratic route. After several hours of following jungle trails, we walked out of a tree line, over two fairly low hills, and across a flat open area. Behind the tree line on the other side stood a well-hidden hootch. This was the first structure we saw of a camp compound set on a hillside and carved into an area concealed by a canopy of trees that camouflaged the camp from overflying aircraft. When I walked into the compound, I was disheartened. Conditioned by the old war movies I had seen back home, I had expected to find walls, guard towers, cells with beds, and the aroma of cooking food. All I saw was an extension of the jungle.

Our Sleeping Quarters

The camp itself was about two hundred yards long and 150 yards wide in all, including the living quarters for the camp commander, the cadre, and the guards. An almost dry stream trickled by the edge of the camp. The prisoners' enclosure was maybe sixty yards by ninety yards, set off with a bamboo fence and gateway. Four small huts, one of which housed the prisoners, stood within the enclosure, and a latrine pit was at one corner. Inside the hootch where we would stay we found an eight-foot by twelve-foot pallet of split bamboo, standing three feet from the floor, that had served as the "bed" for four men. Now it would have to sleep the seven newcomers as well. That was the hard, unforgiving surface that we would sleep on for the duration of our captivity in the jungle. As a result, we suffered terrible bed sores, welts, and bruises. There would be no mats, blankets, or mosquito nets. Months would pass before we would see even those few amenities. Outside, just beyond the fence and behind the huts, a threatening row of punji stakes—sharpened bamboo stakes smeared with excrement to assure serious infection if they pierced the skin of a man trying to escape—had been driven into the ground and pointed inward from the perimeter.

Tall trees grew all around the area, with some pulled over to break the hootches' outline and conceal them from spotter planes. The entire camp was set within an almost impenetrable jungle of ferns, vines, bamboo thickets, wild banana trees, hardwoods, and other tropical vegetation. The jungle floor was thick with brush and hip-high ferns. Broadleaf trees of medium height grew above the floor, and huge hardwoods arched more than one hundred feet high and interlaced to form a great green shroud to hide the camp from searching eyes above.

At the entrance to the compound, we were met by a nasty dispositioned Vietnamese who identified himself as "Mr. Huoung" and who spoke passable English. He was to be our interpreter. The American prisoners, having difficulty with the pronunciation of his name, dubbed him "Mr. Holmes" for the duration of our unpleasant acquaintance. Holmes broke into a tirade, haranguing us, "Stand at attention! You are at the prison for American war criminals!" I mumbled, "Aw shit, you've got to be kidding," my loose, sarcastic tongue once again overpowering my judgment and good sense. Holmes yelled in response, "You! You stand at attention! I did not give you permission to speak!" When we shuffled our feet, he grew even angrier. "You will be allowed to meet the other prisoners. But if you do not obey the rules, you will be punished severely."

With that grim introduction, we were led through the bamboo gate into the prisoners' enclosure. Inside was a thin American, Russell Grissett, a marine and

Sketch of Viet Cong POW Camp Drawn by Frank Anton during his Debrief after Release

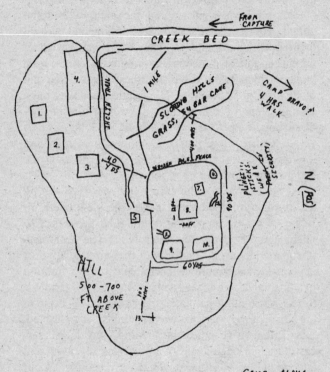

CAMP ALPHA

1 Cadre Billets	8 Six POWs
2 Cadre Billets	9 POW Hut (Not Used)
3 Cadre Kitchen	10 POW Hut (Not Used)
4 Meeting Hall/Classroom	11 1967 (On Tree)
5 Guard Post	12 Water Supply Shallow Creek,
6 Latrine Mound	Polluted and Almost Dry
7 Three ARVN POWs	13 Grave Site of Eisenbrown

one of four Americans being held in the camp. He had on black pajama bottoms rolled up to his knees. He was bare-chested, and every rib showed through his skin. His hair, filthy dirty and blond, had been cut short on the sides, Vietnamese style, but it was long in the front. He told us that he had been a prisoner for two years. Two years, I said to myself as I looked at the barren ground of the prisoners' living area, the spare conditions, and the filth. I couldn't live in here for two months! Grissett was very happy to see us, jabbering on for half an hour with small talk, asking what was going on back in the "world," how the war was going, and other trivia.

Freedom So Soon

Then Grissett told us, "There's gonna be a release ceremony tomorrow. We're gonna eat full, lots of pig meat." He explained that two Puerto Rican U.S. Army enlisted men were being set free, which was always an occasion for a banquet. That news instantly encouraged us. *Released?* Grissett said that many ARVNs had been set free last year. A banquet had preceded that release also. Our minds were fixed on that one word, *released*.

That night, no one slept. Around a barely smoldering campfire, we each in turn told our life stories and the details of our captures. We seven new prisoners were joined by Grissett and two of the Americans already being held in the camp, Capt. Floyd Kushner, an army flight surgeon whom we naturally soon began calling "Doc," and Bob Sherman, a marine. The fourth man we would meet the next day.

As Grissett had promised, the release ceremony began the following day. The occasion was filled with speeches by the camp commander and cadre praising the two "progressive" Puerto Ricans for having demonstrated proper contrition for their aggression against the innocent Vietnamese people in their struggle for liberation from the puppet government in the south. It took me awhile to realize that every speech, every exaggeration of praise for the soon-to-be-released prisoners was also directed at the rest of us in an effort to coerce our submission to the mind games they were playing. That awakening would come from hard experience in the weeks, months, and years to come, but I found myself caught up in the excitement of the ceremonies, especially the promise of a feast.

Grissett had been right. We were ushered to a huge bamboo table in the center of the compound built just for the occasion. Large bowls of rice, fruit, and vegetables were placed before us. Then smaller bowls appeared, some filled with chunks of boiled pig meat, others with cubes of pig fat, still others with dark red hunks of a coagulated substance that Grissett told us later was pig blood. We newcomers gazed up and down the table, more than a little apprehensive. That was when we caught sight of the other American, a marine named Earl Clyde Weatherman. We found it odd that he was sitting up front with the Vietnamese. This oddity grew a great deal stranger as we continued to puzzle over Weatherman's status in the months to come.

While we new prisoners sat wide-eyed at the curiosity before us, Grissett, Weatherman, and Sherman acted as men possessed. All three gorged themselves as if it was to be their last meal. They crammed piece after piece of the pig meat into their already stuffed cheeks. When the meat was gone, they devoured the blood and cleaned out the bowls of pig fat. By then, the Vietnamese cooks had brought out more bowls of meat and blood, and they grabbed for more. Only when those bowls were empty and no more were forthcoming did they eat any of the rice, vegetables, or fruit. None of us newly captured Americans had seen, or even imagined, such a spectacle. Kushner, who had been a prisoner for only a couple of months, was more selective. He hastily ate the meat, but when it was gone he turned to the rice and vegetables. He tasted a small bit of the blood, then went back to the rice and soon called it quits.

What we were witnessing was shocking. After our two and a half weeks of captivity, we were certainly hungry, but we weren't that hungry! Around the campfire that night, Grissett gave us a crash course in celebrations. He told us that such chances to "eat full" were going to be very few and far between. We would see meat only a few times a year, and we had better take advantage of those rare celebrations if we wanted to stay alive with any hope of ever making it out of that POW camp. He was right. The entire group of us would not see meat again for months, and when we did, we knew exactly how to conduct ourselves.

By then, Ortiz-Rivera and Santos had been released and were following their guard—escorts to freedom. Kushner had managed to slip a note to one of them with our names on it in hopes that word could be gotten back to our families that we were alive. Before the two men left amid ample propaganda fanfare, the Vietnamese had outfitted them in clean white pajamas with a bright red sash draped across their chests. Holmes made yet another political speech, and Grissett delivered one of his own about how he needed to "do better" about being "progressive" so that he, too, could be released.

When we went back to our area of the camp, Grissett was really downcast. That was when he told us about the need to know how to take care of ourselves. The rest of us, though, were elated as hell. In one day they were already releasing people! It never occurred to us that night that they had delayed the release until we had arrived to exert the maximum psychological effect on us. We soon became aware that Grissett was subject to severe swings in his moods. The next day, for example, he was very upbeat. He told us that the Vietnamese could read minds, and it became clear in the weeks to come that he had lost his. Sherman was another mystery, alternating in moods between easygoing and morose. Grissett later told us that Sherman had been working in the marine morgue with body bags and had gone "nuts" long before his capture. He had begun to see all his buddies being stuffed into those body bags, and he "lost it." As for Weatherman, he too was a mystery. When we had a chance to encounter him that first day by the stream that ran by the edge of the camp, he had said, "I'm Earl Weatherman. Don't believe everything you hear about me." We had already seen him sitting in the company of our captors, and we weren't sure what to think, regardless of what we heard.

Although not yet fully evident to us, these three men were an indication of the effect that jungle captivity can have on men. They were gaunt, but though they appeared to be physically able to survive their harsh conditions, their minds were suspect. These troubled, tortured men were a sad preview of the harrowing years that I could not foresee nor could I prevent.

5
Decline of Body and Soul

Of the 591 U.S. prisoners of war officially accounted for during Operation Homecoming in 1973, as America withdrew from the war in Southeast Asia, only 102 had spent at least part of their captivity in the jungles of the south. The vast number of the others, primarily air force and navy pilots, had been confined in the north, generally in or around Hanoi.

All seventy-seven of those from the army were taken prisoner during operations in the south. A great deal of resentment built among a handful of those—especially some of the aviators—who had spent their entire captivity in Hanoi, when they learned that those of us who had spent years in the south considered our transfer to Hanoi to be a virtual reprieve. They were especially bitter and angry at a comment I and a couple of others had made that the Hanoi prison, compared with our jungle camp, was like a Holiday Inn, because in Hanoi nobody starved, and nobody was worked to death. At the same time, I know that many of the men held in Hanoi, especially those captured before 1968, suffered immensely from horrible torture at the hands of their cruel and savage captors.

Army Capt. Floyd Kushner, who had spent two months longer in jungle captivity than I had, said with some bitterness after his return home, "I've heard about solitary confinement, and I've heard about being put in cells, and I've heard about poor food. I want to tell you I was damn glad to get to North Vietnam. I thought it was splendid. It was so easy being in jail and getting a couple of meals of bread and soup a day. I could have survived there for fifty years, but in South Vietnam I couldn't."

His comments were not well received by the commissioned officers who had spent longer times in the Hanoi system and considered themselves better educated, better trained, and better disciplined than what they must have assumed was the "rabble" from the south. Some of them even suggested that the high death rate among us was a result of our being incompetent, undisciplined, and leaderless. I refused then, and I refuse now, to allow such wrongheaded assertions that would condemn, trivialize, or ignore the gruesome ordeal we lived through to go unchallenged.

This is not to say that life in the north did not hold its own form of agony arising from close, dehumanizing confinement, fear of the heavy bombing that rained down mercilessly in and around Hanoi, and the constant, bitter uncertainty about our fate. Without question, many of the pilots were tortured unmercifully. Navy Capt. Eugene "Red" McDaniel was almost tortured to death, and a few others died from a combination of their wounds after being shot down and the cruel punishment at the hands of the North

Vietnamese. Except for several pilots who were brutally tortured after an escape attempt from the Hanoi Hilton in 1969, such barbarity was not the norm by the time I had arrived in Hanoi in August 1971.

Compared with the conditions we had experienced in the south, the food was better and more plentiful, but it was still bad and insufficient. The two years that I spent in Hanoi were indeed awful. But life in the south, for those blessed enough to make it out, was a nightmare of hellish proportions that transformed civilized human beings into primal animals struggling to cling to some fleeting sense of what it means to be alive, and why. In some, that tiny ember of hope finally flickered out. At best, it was a half-life because of the traumatic and debilitating experience of having survived the malnutrition, disease, and near insanity that had ultimately killed so many of our fellow prisoners who never lived to make it north, much less make it home as we did.

An Unspeakable Existence

For three years, I was a member of a group that eventually came to number a total of twenty-four Americans who suffered an unspeakable existence in the jungle. The most compelling testimony of what we endured lies in the fact that, except for one man who was believed killed trying to escape in April 1968, and three men who were released by our captors in late October 1969, only twelve of us survived until 1971, when we walked about five hundred miles out of South Vietnam, along the Ho Chi Minh trail through Laos, and into North Vietnam.

During the three years in the south, we were confined in four permanent camps, all of which were similar: built on heavily forested hillsides, a stream running near or through the compound area, and the similar bamboo and thatch hootches set off from the rest of the camp by a bamboo fence. We never knew the exact location of the camps, hidden as they were in the thick jungle. Our relatively small number of eleven men who had witnessed the release of the two Puerto Ricans in late January quickly began to grow by twos and threes, so that by August 1968, there were twenty-one of us falling into varying stages of illness. During the rainy season, downpours continued for weeks on end, leaving the camp a slimy wallow of mud mixed with human excrement left where the dysentery-stricken men stood because they could not reach the latrine pit in time.

For the first several months, even during the dry season, we had to walk barefoot through that stinking filth because the guards refused to allow us any sandals. I found myself fighting the despair that comes with hunger and the helplessness of physical and mental incapacitation. As more prisoners were brought into the camp, our total ration of food—three small cups a day of filthy, vermin-ridden rice laced with rat droppings—was not increased. By March, each man's portion had been cut in half, and it was to become worse as more prisoners were brought into the camp.

In our weakened condition, the guards knew that any thought of escape was doomed, not only because we lacked the physical strength but also because the jungle itself was forbidding. And each camp was within a short distance of Montagnard tribesmen who lusted to kill Americans who had bombed their villages, poisoned their crops with chemicals, and killed their family members. We were not just prisoners of the Vietnamese but of the jungle as well.

These conditions began a gradual assault not only on our increasingly frail bodies but also on our minds and souls. As bad as the physical infirmities were, nothing had prepared us for the mental and emotional trauma of having encountered a "white gook" who had become the enemy.

Meet the "White Gook"

Russ Grissett, who met us when we arrived at the first permanent camp, had told us of Bobby Garwood, a marine who had been captured near Da Nang in 1965, two and a half years earlier. For the next eighteen months, Garwood would act as interpreter, spy, guard, and informant on the prisoners who had once been his comrades in arms. He had made his own separate peace, and by making it at our expense, he had subjected us to yet another realm of despair and sense of betrayal that made our captivity all the more unbearable.

Garwood's treachery was most pronounced a few months later, in June, when he participated in a political indoctrination course with the Vietnamese who tried to break us of our political "sins." Garwood had gone so far as to suggest that "successful" completion of the course would lead to release for the most "progressive" among us. It was but another cruel betrayal, and the devastating psychological blow led directly and quickly to the ruination of two of our fellow prisoners. Before Thanksgiving, six prisoners had died.

By August 1968, a terrible skin disease had infected most of us, leading several to the brink of insanity. The agony only further complicated the already serious cases of malaria and dysentery that were draining our bodies of strength and gradually snuffing out the will to live among many of us, myself included. When the prisoners began dying in rapid succession that fall, I felt that I had come to dwell in the darkest, most despairing corner of hell.

Resentment and animosity began to surface among the prisoners because those who were strong enough to carry wood for the cooking fire and to carry loads of *manioc*, a potato-like vegetable, to supplement our paltry ration of rice began to hold it against the weakened, listless men who could barely stand, much less walk. I understood their feelings because I was among the sickest. Those who could work were also stricken and miserable, and being forced to endure a disproportionate share of the labor left the group vulnerable to divisions. There were times when everybody thought everybody hated each other, which played right into the hands of the Vietnamese who would stop at almost nothing to divide us from each other and exploit our weaknesses. The greatest contributing factor to the hostility that sprang up in our midst, though, was sickness. Some were just sicker than others, but all of us had regressed to the point of relying on animal instincts merely to survive. And some of us eventually lost the ability to do that.

Anger Prevailed

These miseries, coupled with seeing Garwood living better than we did and spying on us, put the entire camp in a state of heightened anger that led us to turn on each other to some extent. We had been prepared to go into battle and risk being wounded or even killed. None of us, though, had been prepared to become prisoners of war under the horrifyingly desperate conditions that we found ourselves in. And we certainly had not been prepared to be captured and then subjected to that barbarity at the hands of an American who had crossed to the other side. That was a form of torture all by itself.

6
Camp One

During the first two and a half weeks of captivity, I had no way of knowing that what the seven of us were experiencing was relatively mild in comparison with what was to come. Any hunger I felt was of my own doing because I refused to eat the rice. The guards, although they were always pressing us to move at a hurried pace to avoid detection when we were on the trail, were contemptuous of us but not physically brutal. We were not beaten or seriously mistreated physically during those first couple of weeks, probably because the guards were eager to move us to the security of a well-hidden prison camp and knew that cripples could not make very good time.

I wasn't aware of it at the time, but in mid- to late 1967, Ho Chi Minh had ordered a policy of capturing as many U.S. servicemen as possible to leverage concessions from Washington. This concerted policy produced an escalating number of prisoners in the years to come, a fortunate change for many of us because Americans often had been routinely executed at the time of their capture. They not only were killed by the VC and NVA but also by villagers in isolated areas where unfortunate pilots would drift into their hands after parachuting from damaged aircraft. I don't think I ever considered myself lucky at the time to have been taken prisoner, but after reflection since then, I know the consequences could have been a lot worse. And, as the last two decades have demonstrated, the long-standing Vietnamese policy of using prisoners as collateral created a bitterly divisive situation in the United States that continues today.

After all these years, the suspicion lingers that not all the men held prisoner returned from the war, and some, in fact, may still be somewhere in Southeast Asia under Hanoi's control.

A Troublesome Train

Although I was hungry and beginning to feel the onset of weakness from a self-imposed diet of no more than a few occasional bananas, I still had enough spunk to "mouth off" occasionally to my captors, who didn't fully understand my snide, profane insults in English slang. This trait, I was to learn later, would be a source of trouble when I was within earshot of an interpreter or a camp officer who understood me.

By the time we arrived at the first permanent prison compound and were met with the high-pitched harangues of "Mr. Holmes," most of the seven of us were still in tolerable condition. Both Army 1st Sgt. Richard Williams and Army Cpl. Francis Cannon, casualties from the Delta Company ambush a few days after my shoot-down, had been wounded but could pretty well keep up on the walk through the jungle. After our brief introduction and our meeting with Russ Grissett, the promise of a "banquet" had left us with the notion that we could tolerate the ordeal. Despite the disgusting meal of blood and pig fat, we ate fairly well of the lean meat and other "edible" food put before us, and the release the next day of the Puerto Ricans actually raised our hopes that freedom for us was probably going to happen sooner rather than later.

But no sooner had the released men disappeared in their clean white pajamas and red sashes, waving back to us as they headed for freedom, than the guards ordered Grissett and Robert Lewis, my crew chief, to begin carrying the cooking utensils to a new camp. We learned that such moves were routine and immediate after a prisoner release to prevent any rescue attempts of those left behind. "Camp Two" was being prepared in anticipation of freeing the Puerto Ricans, and the Vietnamese wasted little time in making the switch. Before we left, though, the guards brought in several medics to work on Williams's and Cannon's wounds. That was our first indication that any medical care we were likely to receive would be primitive at best, and certainly provided grudgingly. by the VC quacks who detested us.

The Vietnamese refused to acknowledge Capt. Floyd Kushner as the doctor he was. After his capture in December 1967, he had spent about two months with Grissett and the other two marines, Earl Clyde Weatherman and Bob Sherman, in the camp where I first arrived. The VC, though, forced him to sit by helplessly while the medics applied their crude, in-

competent, and clumsy treatment. Williams's
wounded hand was turning black, and one of the VC
medics said that the arm would have to be amputated.
But we knew that wasn't going to happen with no
anesthesia available, and for good measure Williams
lied by saying that he had a heart condition. That
persuaded the medic to treat the wound with penicillin
and leave it at that. So a couple of us removed Williams's filthy, smelly bandages and took them to the
nearly dry creek to wash them and hang them to dry.
Several weeks later, in an odd quirk of nature, mag-
gots invaded the wound. After they had devoured
every bit of dead, infected flesh, they disappeared
from his body as quickly as they had arrived and
never returned.

Cannon's wounds got equally shabby treatment
from the VC medics. He had taken some shrapnel in
his back during the firefight where Delta Company
got routed. He had had a dressing applied a couple
of days before by a nurse at the hootch along the trail
where he, Williams, Dave Harker, and Jim Strickland
had joined Lewis, Pfister, and me. By then, almost his
entire back had become a big, ugly abscess. The nurse
mashed on it and squeezed a flow of pus from the
raw flesh, then shoved a cotton-tipped instrument beneath the skin to swab out the rancid-smelling wound.
The medic who changed the bandage in the camp was
equally callous in his treatment. Through it all, Cannon barely flinched from the obvious pain.

That afternoon, Grissett and Lewis returned to tell
us that the camp would not be ready for us until the
next day. The walk would take about six hours, they
said. We tried, without much success, to get some
sleep that night, stuffed together as we were on the

hard bamboo pallet and anxious about what lay ahead the next day. The guards herded us out at about seven o'clock the next morning along a trail that crossed over several heavily forested hills. Captivity had begun to take a toll, especially on the wounded, and stragglers followed along behind the rest of us until they caught up at one of the numerous Montagnard villages along the way.

As morning wore on, the heat began to intensify, and by the time we reached a shallow, rocky stream several hours later, I was beginning to feel the fatigue. We walked in the creek for maybe a quarter-mile, following it up the mountainside. Then, barely visible through the thick foliage, a hootch appeared just beyond the edge of the creek bed. The bank rose about twenty feet, and we walked up steps that had been cut into the steep incline and within a few yards passed through the bamboo fence of the next compound, which I designated Camp Two.

It wasn't really all that much different in appearance from Camp One, also built on a hillside, but the jungle cover was thicker and the stream was deeper and ran more swiftly. Prisoners were confined to bamboo and thatch hootches behind a bamboo fence. The ARVN prisoners were kept apart from us, in a hootch beyond the fence around the U.S. enclosure. For some reason, Weatherman, the marine whose mysterious behavior left us wondering whether he was a crossover to the VC or was just playing along to save his own hide, was to stay with the ARVNs for awhile before being moved in with us. A guard station—actually nothing more than a tiny open hut with a thatch roof to keep the rain off the guard—stood about twenty feet in front of the gate to the prisoner's

Sketch of Viet Cong POW Camp Drawn by Frank Anton during his Debrief after Release

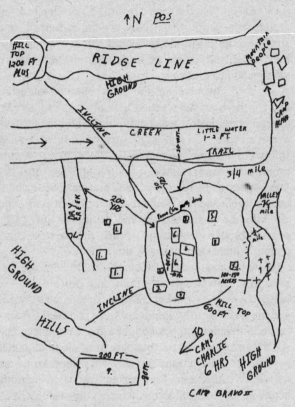

1 Cadre Billets	6 US POWs
2 Guard	7 Unused Building
4 Cadre Kitchen	8 Stock Houses
4 Medical	9 Open Field, Corn
5 ARVN POWs	and Orange

area. The camp commander, guards, and cadre had quarters about a hundred yards or so in separate locations up the hill from our area.

A Dilution of Rations

Camp Two, embedded somewhere in the low mountains in the western part of Vietnam and somewhere east of Laos, became the setting for a horror story that lasted for fifteen months. By April 1968, our numbers began to increase as new prisoners were brought into the camp. The ration of rice that at first provided for eleven men then had to feed twenty. The first to arrive was Bill Port, who had been seriously wounded in January and spent a month in a VC hospital before he was transferred to Camp Two. The "miracles" of Viet Cong medicine evidently were useless to help him. In early March, five others came in. Army enlisted men James Daly and Willie Watkins were in Alpha Company, which had met the same fate as Charlie and Delta companies in a similar ambush in the same general area of the Que Son Valley. Three marine enlisted men—Denny Hammond, Joe Zawtocki, and Fred Burns—were captured in separate incidents. All five came into the camp under guard and the watchful eye of Bobby Garwood, who carried an AK-47 assault rifle and was dressed in the same garb as the Vietnamese. That was the first time that we had seen Garwood, although Grissett had told us something about him during our short stay in Camp One.

Later that month, two more army enlisted men arrived: Ike McMillan and Thomas Davis. Julius Long came in May. Within four months, our numbers had almost doubled, which meant that each man's portion of food had been cut almost in half. The daily rations at first amounted to nothing but rice—the inferior red variety that even the poorest Vietnamese ate only to fend off starvation and usually fed to their pigs. Most often the aged sacks containing the rice had been buried in a cache for God knows how long to conceal it while the VC carried on their interminable guerrilla war. The pittance that the guards poured out from a dirty metal container each day for the prisoners was infested with bugs and rat feces. And as our hunger began to blunt our strength and our senses, we soon neglected the simple routine of sifting the disease-bearing filth from the rice.

Almost from the outset, Floyd Kushner, the flight surgeon who was already in Camp One when we arrived, did his best to encourage us to do everything possible to maintain our health. In this, which was to become our "death camp," he never stopped giving us small but critical bits of advice. He urged everyone to keep alive by eating all of that miserable food we were able to obtain. He had dying men virtually force-fed, usually a futile attempt, but it was all we could do for them under the circumstances. In my case, at least, it worked. When the rations were cut by the VC, he hounded the camp commander to give us more food and other rations. He persisted in arguing that we needed more medicine, and on those rare occasions when they brought him some, he managed to hide and hoard it, holding it back for the times when it might keep someone alive, if only for a week or even a day.

He also prodded us to try to keep ourselves as clean as possible. Every day that the guards would let him, Kushner would make himself trudge down to the stream to bathe. Rarely did we have access to a bar of the crude lye soap, but even without it he would force his body to endure the arduous journey down the steep embankment to the cold stream that served as the bathing area. What had at first been a few-minutes walk soon became a struggle. After a month or so, it took ten minutes to walk the two hundred yards, and after another month it was as much as forty minutes. Leaning on a homemade walking stick to support him, out of breath and strength after only three or four steps, he forced himself down the steep embankment and then made the even more difficult trip back up. He kept doing it, and he kept pleading with the rest of us to follow his example.

Some, myself included, didn't heed the advice as well as we should have. Both my knees had been smashed up in my chopper crash, and several vertebrae had become compressed. Combined with the sickness and malnutrition, I found my will to survive quickly challenged. By the fall of 1968, when people started dying, my will became weaker still. As my health and that of others plummeted toward rockbottom, I stopped eating regularly, stopped bathing, and stopped even caring. I refused to climb off the hard bamboo bed but would just sit in an almost catatonic state. I sat like that for hours, days, and weeks at a time. In my addled mind, this seemed to be a comforting distraction.

Julius Long somehow had kept an army poncho liner after he was captured, and the two of us would cover ourselves and sit under its shelter for almost an entire day, refusing to come out except to eat. The trancelike state became so appealing that in time I lost even the desire to come out to eat. Other prisoners

would reason with me, prod me for some reaction,
some movement, but I simply didn't care anymore.
"Fuck it," I would say. "We're all gonna die anyway,
so what's the difference?"

Somebody Had to Work

That attitude did nothing to improve the morale of the
men. Just because we were held in a guarded compound did not mean that we simply lay around all the
time. There was work to do. To cook our meager
rations of rice, we needed wood, and each day the
guards would take out a detail for woodgathering. The
incessant rains not only compounded our misery but
also made finding dry wood difficult, forcing us to
venture farther and farther away, further sapping our
energy.

Our food also was supplemented with *manioc*, the
bland, potato-like plant that the prisoners were sent
in work crews to dig up and haul back to camp in
large baskets. Each load weighed about seventy
pounds, and the *manioc* runs could cover a distance
of two or three miles. Obviously, this hard labor was
beyond the ability of many of us in the camp, and
those who were strong enough to do it became angry
and resentful that they were having to do all the work
of feeding the group. As it happened, the strongest
among us were three blacks: Willie Watkins, Ike Mc-
Millan, and Tom Davis.

Watkins had been with Alpha Company when he
and Daly were captured on January 9, 1968. A third
man taken with them died of his wounds and was
buried in the jungle near the trail. Watkins was a native of South Carolina where he grew up during the

turbulent years of the civil rights movement of the 1950s and 1960s. His stories around our campfires invariably summoned memories of police dogs and fire hoses being turned on local black people. He also had recollections of lynchings. His background had made him tough and strong willed. That strength led to conflict with some of the other, weaker prisoners, and on a few occasions it resulted in his physically asserting himself when he was convinced others were refusing to carry their share of the work. Yet his ability to prevail over his own sickness and to press others to do more to contribute to the well-being of the group had the effect, whether Watkins intended it or not, of forcing many of us to keep on living.

Davis was another pillar of strength. A native of Eufala, Alabama, he also drew on the trying circumstances of a black man growing up in rural America to persevere against the trials of jungle survival. Although he suffered a tooth abscess throughout his captivity, he managed to convey a sense of humor that, if not always infectious, at least helped others not to surrender to despair.

McMillan was the consummate adapter. No matter how brutal the situation became, he found a way to adjust without too much complaint. He was a mortar crewman from Gretna, Florida, and his attitude seemed to be to accept the hand that life had dealt him and just work through it a day at a time. He was also a great thief, skilled at purloining extra rations of rice. Once he stole a four-pound slab of pork, and his knack for stealing the guards' chickens was a source of grateful amazement for us and a mystery to the guards. McMillan got sick like everyone else, but he also seemed to recover within a few days to continue working and assisting other prisoners.

Watkins eventually became the de facto camp leader because he was strongest in body and will. He, McMillan, and Davis seemed especially resilient. For some reason, although they were also stricken with malaria and dysentery, they were able to shake off the effects in a way that most of the white men from city backgrounds could not, although David Harker and Jim Strickland also were able to do more than their share of the work. Watkins and the other blacks often accused those who didn't work of being lazy slackers and at times threatened to keep a larger share of the food for themselves. Those, like me, who began to feel guilty about not doing more work, also felt help-less to convince our fellow prisoners of how sick and weak we really were. This created a source of deep division within the camp, and even though it was not a purely racial tension, that element of our discord was never far from the surface. Only when men began to die by September did the anger partially give way to our common struggle for survival.

In the meantime, Kushner did what he could to try to keep the group focused on the very act of living. As a doctor, he knew the importance of establishing a discipline that would help forestall the deterioration that was predictable under the hostile conditions of a prison camp. Those efforts, though, were made under difficult circumstances. Kushner was the only doctor captured during the Vietnam War, and he had been stripped by the VC of any authority. He had been captured in late November 1967, when his helicopter crashed into a hilltop one night after he had attended a lecture in Da Nang, ironically, on the dangers of night flying. The pilot was killed instantly in the fiery crash, and the copilot was seriously wounded. Kushner stayed with the injured man while the crew chief left on foot to find help. He never returned. After a couple of days, Kushner decided to leave the scene and seek aid. From the bottom of the hill, he looked back up to see choppers circling the crash site, but by the time he could scramble back up the hill, he was alone and was captured soon afterward.

A medical intern at Tripler Army Medical Center in Hawaii, Kushner had volunteered for combat duty only months earlier. He had left his wife and a newborn baby girl at home in Virginia. The crash had injured his shoulder and left him in severe pain. And after being placed in the camp with Grissett, Sherman, and Weatherman, he began to contract the jungle diseases that were so destructive to his health and his mental well-being. Compounding his agony was the pain and suffering of the other prisoners whom he was helpless to assist except in the most rudimentary way. He helped them secretly to avoid being punished for breaking the camp commander's rules.

The Viet Cong refused to allow us to recognize either his rank as a commissioned officer or his medical profession—demands that were another calculated design to break our morale and any semblance of organization for resistance. For the first couple of years, they even ordered us not to refer to him as "Doc," so he became simply Kush. As an army doctor, he had not been trained for command, and, as a warrant officer, neither had I. So the classic prisoner of war military structure never had a chance in our camp. "Top" Williams, the first sergeant from Delta Company who had been wounded in the hand, was the ranking enlisted man and was by far the most experienced in military matters. Williams, at forty-one, was also the oldest. He had been captured in the second week of January 1968, while sweeping through the area of our shoot-down to search for us and other survivors from the ambush. His unit was hit by an overpowering NVA force, and despite his wounded hand, he held off the attack with a courageous stand during which he fired his M-79 grenade launcher repeatedly into the oncoming enemy, killing at least a dozen. Eventually, the superior numbers overcame the Delta Company survivors, and Williams was taken prisoner along with Harker, Strickland, and Cannon.

Williams had seen heavy combat in Korea as well as Vietnam and had been all over the world. So for awhile he was able to assert a sort of informal authority simply on the basis that he had lived longer and seen more. At first, he lifted everyone's spirits with his determined assurances, "This war will come to an end, we'll all get out of here. There will be a POW exchange, there always is." But his wound and growing weakness from sickness prevented him from filling the void of a command structure that never formed. And the VC took advantage of it. The only authority that Kushner had was the respect we held for his knowledge and for the courage of his example—as long as he was well enough to provide it. And the Vietnamese made certain that would quickly become almost impossible. He was isolated, tied up, beaten, shackled, and denied the freedom to provide medical care for his fellow prisoners.

On the Road to Starvation

But there was nothing Kushner or anyone else could do about the rapid decline in the prisoners' health from the malnutrition that quickly began to set in among us. Lack of nutrients in the starvation-level quantities of rice we ate stunted the growth of our hair and nails and contributed to an overall susceptibility to a whole range of disease and other ailments common to the jungle. The tiny ration of rice was supplemented only by *manioc*, a few edible greens, and a fish sauce called *nuoc mam* that smelled and tasted like rotten fish offal.

The guards tried to give us the impression that they were living on the same sparse diet as the prisoners, but they not only had plenty of the higher quality white rice but also chicken and eggs to provide the protein that made the difference between starvation and survival. At most, we received tiny portions of chicken or pig meat once every four to six months, and the consequences were devastating.

Almost from the beginning, malaria and dysentery began to infect the prisoners. The vitamin deficiency caused all of us to suffer scurvy, osteomalacia, bleeding gums, gingivitis, edema, and lost teeth. For more than a year, we had no shoes or clothing other than the flimsy black pajamas worn by the Vietnamese to replace the fatigues that eventually rotted away from our bodies. We went barefoot for several months and received no blankets to ward off the rain-drenched chill of the mountains except for worn-out, discarded rice sacks with the faded imprint, "Donated by the People of the U.S.A.," which had been roughly sewn together. Because we had no mosquito nets, the swarms of huge insects literally sucked away our juices and deposited the germs that infected each of us with malaria. The VC withheld quinine, one of the few drugs available, until we had been exposed for long periods of time and were in serious danger of dying. Even then, the quantities of the medicine were inadequate to make a substantial improvement in our conditions.

All the men suffered from acute and chronic dysentery. Our systems were so afflicted that each man had to defecate between sixty and a hundred times a day. The latrines were as much as a quarter-mile away, and more times than not we never made it that far. Our clothes became detestable, and the compound was like a barnyard, strewn with piles and puddles of human excrement that we walked through in our bare feet because we were simply too sick to clean it up. Disease fed on disease.

Around the first of April, 1968, after the diseases had begun to wear the men down but before they became deathly serious, we had settled into a routine of gathering firewood, *manioc*, and as many other edible plants as we could find. These forays placed us in close contact with our Vietnamese guards, who were a cross-section of humanity. For the most part, they treated us like human beings, or at least as well as could be expected under wartime circumstances. A few, however, I would have killed in a heartbeat.

One in particular was an ugly little man we nick-named "Frankenstein" because of his facial appearance as well as the way he walked, with a stiff, bowlegged shuffle. He was so cruel that even some of the other guards despised him. His mean streak, though, was as wide as his intellect was narrow. Frankenstein loved to fish—not with the traditional pole, line, and hook but with hand grenades, the unreliable chicom variety made in China. He would toss the grenade into a fishing hole, the concussion would stun or kill the fish, and Frankenstein would wade in and gather the bountiful catch. One day he made the mistake of taking an American-made grenade that he had found to the stream. U.S. fragmentation grenades were far superior in every respect to the chicoms that Frankenstein was accustomed to using for bait. He was blown to smithereens. The peculiar circumstances of his demise became the source of great amusement to the other guards, who laughed hysterically. We, though, were careful to reserve our muted merriment for times when the guards were not within hearing.

A Humane Guard

Another of the guards was named Quang, an amiable enough young man who always pestered us to help him with his English. He said that he had taught English to children in Hanoi, but that his repeated critical statements about the conduct of the war in the south had resulted in his being drafted and sent to study the subject firsthand. His ability to speak English was a break that took him out of the line units and placed him guarding American POWs. He was as humane as any of the guards, and we rewarded his leniency with instruction in the nuances of the language, especially the slang and swearwords.

One day Quang came into our hootch with a perplexed expression on his face. One phrase had confused him, and he asked for clarification. "When you

Americans are very angry at something, you say 'mother fuck.' Would it therefore be proper that when you are very, very, very angry to then say 'father fuck'?" Hardly able to retain a straight face, I blurted out to him, "Absolutely, Quang! But you must remember that 'father fuck' must only be used in an extreme situation where you would be terribly angry." The explanation seemed to satisfy him, and I can recall only once when he used the phrase, and then with great relish and profane emphasis.

Actually, Quang's true loyalties were always a little suspect because he liked to daydream about America. He was fascinated with Cadillacs, Rolex watches, and *Playboy* magazine, all fruits of American imperialist materialism that his superiors detested. One day, while Quang was guarding us as we gathered wood, we asked him what he would do if a U.S. helicopter landed in that field right then. "Why, I'd get on it with all of you and go to America." Then he smiled, and I truly think he was serious.

Camp rules required the prisoners to bow to the guards as a sign of respect and deference. I considered it to be an act of demeaning submission and generally tried to avoid contact with the guards as much as possible. In the early spring of 1968, I was returning from the bathing area at the stream with Kushner and Strickland. As usual, I was lagging behind, and when I caught up with them at the gate to the compound, a guard had blocked their entry. He uttered some words in Vietnamese, which no one understood, so we stood there confused.

From inside the fence, Grissett appeared and said something in Vietnamese to the guard, who answered brusquely. "He wants you to bow," Grissett said. So

Kushner and Strickland nodded slightly toward the guard, who returned the "bow" with a similar bob of his head and let them pass. I started to walk in behind them, but the guard, no more than nineteen, stepped in front of me and brandished his rifle. My rebellious side decided to buck the rules, so I glared deep into the young guard's eyes and with all the couth and grace I had learned in the U.S. Army, I said, "Fuck you." Unfortunately, that was one of the few phrases in his command of English. He pointed his rifle at my chest and spit out some words I could not understand, and I said, "No! You can shoot me, but I will not bow to you, you young punk!"

Grissett pleaded with me to go through the motions, but I still refused. Then the guard began to open the bayonet on the barrel of his rifle. Now, getting shot would have provided a reasonably quick end to the nightmare of the prison camp, and for some reason I no longer feared being shot. But the thought of being stabbed with that rusty blade and left to bleed slowly to death scared the hell out of me. I bowed immediately, not once but five or six times, and then slid around him into the compound to the derisive taunts of my fellow prisoners. After that, without any prodding, I always gave that particular gate-keep his little bow.

By spring, hunger had become chronic, and we were always looking for ways to supplement our sparse rations. The food runs for *manioc* were the primary source of such supplements. One day I was returning with three or four other prisoners from one of the gathering expeditions, and we passed through a cornfield owned by the nearby Montagnard village. I dropped behind the others and began to fill my pajama bottoms with the small, three-inch ears of corn.

When we arrived in the village and sat down to rest, someone noticed that I had stuffed some of their corn into my trousers. The villagers erupted in outrage and began poking me with their spears and screaming at me. They tied me up and left me sitting on the ground for more than an hour. Then Garwood walked up, listened to the charges, and told me that they had decided to punish me. They were going to return me to the field, he said, and allow me to eat all the corn that I wanted. As hungry as I was, that seemed like a punishment that I could accept. Then Garwood explained further: They would then spear me to death. After some excited conversation back and forth with Garwood, the villagers decided to release me and return me to the camp. The Vietnamese, through Garwood, must have convinced them that I was more valuable alive than dead. I was placed in the stocks for three days, and the other prisoners shared their rice with me so that I didn't go hungry. I never stole food from the Montagnards again.

As the months passed in 1968, the idea of escape had crossed our minds, but our weakened conditions and the illusion that we could be released within a few months kept us from giving much thought to any concrete plans. One day Zawtocki, Hammond, Sherman, and Daly were sent on a *manioc* run. At the last minute, the mysterious Weatherman volunteered to go along. No one could be sure of his status, and we were suspicious of him. From Grissett we learned that Weatherman had escaped from the brig in Da Nang and was captured soon after. Totally nonpolitical and disgusted with his life in the marines, he convinced the VC that he was willing to join them. He apparently had hoped to work his way into their good graces with some period of service, and in exchange they would let him disappear into Cambodia. For whatever reason, the VC never fully trusted him either, and by the time we came into the camp where we first met him, his loyalties were to neither side— only to himself.

So when the five prisoners finally arrived at the field to begin digging up the *manioc*, Weatherman commented that "it looks like a good day for a bird"—a day to fly away. Only one guard, the detested Frankenstein, was sent to supervise the men. As they were hunched over with their work, Weatherman said to the others that if they could kill the guard and get to the ridgeline to the east, they could make their way to an American infantry unit. Not everyone agreed. Zawtocki refused, and Daly, the man who refused to shoot his rifle even while he was under attack, said that there was no way he could kill the guard. Weatherman decided to act on his own. He walked over to Frankenstein to ask for a drink of water, then he jumped him, wrestling the rifle away from him. Hammond ran over to help hold the guard while Weatherman tossed the rifle to Sherman and told him to shoot him. Sherman said that he couldn't do it and pitched it to Daly, who wouldn't do it. In the confusion, Frankenstein broke away and ran toward the nearby Montagnard village, and at the same instant Weatherman and Hammond began running east. Daly then said that if they didn't beat the guard back to the village, the three remaining prisoners would be in deep trouble. They didn't make it. A hollow gong, more like a trash can lid being whacked with a big stick, began sounding the alarm, and the villagers grabbed spears and old muskets and took off after the escapees. The other three were tied up in the village, and the Montagnards who stayed behind beat them badly.

The rest of us prisoners were unaware that anything was happening. All of a sudden, Garwood came running down to our compound from the cadre hootches yelling for us to stay inside, that a "tiger" was loose, which we thought was peculiar. When the men on the *manioc* run had not returned after about seven hours, we knew that something was wrong. Later that night, guards brought in the beaten Zawtocki, Daly, and Sherman, who told us that Weatherman and Hammond had made a run for it. The next day, Hammond was brought into the camp. He was bloody from severe beatings and had a bullet wound in the back of his leg.

The camp commander announced that he would conduct a "trial" the next day. When it was convened, Hammond admitted that he had tried to escape but that he had never intended to kill the guard. He and Weatherman had run for some distance and found a hiding place near a stream bed. The Montagnards, though, were like bloodhounds and found the two no more than a half hour after they began running. Hammond said that one of the tribesmen aimed his rifle at Weatherman and blew his brains out, killing him instantly. Fearing a similar fate, Hammond began running again, but a bullet in the back of his calf dropped him. He was pushed and shoved back to the village, where the people beat him almost senseless before returning him to the VC guards the next morning.

With his admission of "guilt," Hammond was sentenced to three months in the stocks, an unsheltered bamboo pallet on which he was stretched with his hands in shackles. During that time, he relieved himself where he lay, and fellow prisoners had to bring his water and ration of food to feed him. That ordeal, coupled with the bullet wound, sent Hammond into an irreversible mental decline. For his participation, Sherman was sentenced to one month in the stocks, but Zawtocki and Daly avoided punishment after convincing the camp commander that they had no part in the escape. They were placed on "probation," however, and told that if they broke any rules they would be severely punished.

Rumors persisted, despite Hammond's eyewitness account, that Weatherman either was only wounded or was part of a staged event set up by the Vietnamese to frighten us regarding escape.

7
Death Camp

If we were not exactly certain about weatherman's status among us, we harbored no similar qualms about Bobby Garwood. As soon as we had arrived at Camp One, Russ Grissett told us of an American named "Bob" who had crossed over and was working in several capacities with the Viet Cong. He didn't initially give us many details, but we were to learn from harsh firsthand experience more about Bob.

Garwood, a marine private who had been a driver for officers and other VIPs in Da Nang, had been captured in the fall of 1965, on a road not far from Marble Mountain. According to Grissett, sometime in 1967, Garwood decided to ingratiate himself with the Viet Cong in the hope of gaining their favor. He eventually found himself in a prison camp—our Camp One, as it happened—with Grissett and Army Capt. William F. "Ike" Eisenbraun.

Eisenbraun was a superlative soldier, Special Forces, and a seasoned combat veteran of Korea.

While in captivity, he became almost a father figure
for Garwood, who took his advice and began learning
Vietnamese. Then, without telling Garwood, Eisenbraun and Grissett attempted to escape and were re-
captured. When they returned, and Garwood learned
that he had been left out of the plans, he felt betrayed. Shortly after that, weakened from sickness
and excessive work imposed by the camp guards,
Eisenbraun died and was buried just outside the prisoner compound in September 1967, three and a half
months before we came into the camp. Events leading
to Eisenbraun's death, his relationship with Garwood,
and rough details from Grissett of what transpired before our arrival in January 1968 were our introduction
to Garwood before we ever saw him.

He was the one carrying the AK-47 when Watkins,
Daly, Hammond, Zawtocki, and Burns marched into
Camp Two in March 1968. He walked easily within
the camp, going about as he pleased, and occasionally
he left the camp with a satchel and rifle by himself.
He stayed up the hill with the VC guards and ate with
them, and he was frequently in the company of
Holmes, the de facto camp commander because of his
ability to speak English. We noticed, however, that
for the entire time he was in camp with us he avoided
going near the area where the South Vietnamese
ARVNs were being held. The camp staff had separated the Americans from the ARVNs, placing us in
different compounds in each camp. One of the ARVN
officers, who was named Que, was the equivalent of
an American Special Forces ranger—a tough, ruthless
soldier who was a virulent anticommunist and hated
the enemy. He had a special hatred for Garwood as
well because he had crossed over to the VC. Fearing

that Que would kill him if given half a chance—and I am sure that he would have—Garwood made it a point to avoid going anywhere near the ARVN compounds during the eighteen months he was in our camps.

Garwood the Interpreter

Within days of the arrival of the latest five prisoners, all of us in the camp were brought one at a time to the commander's hootch where we faced Garwood. The conversations were really no more than small talk during this session, with Garwood sitting next to the commander as his translator. Basically, we were there for an attitude check, answering such general questions as, "How do you feel?" and "What do you think about the war?" We had met Garwood first as a weapon-bearing guard, and now we saw him as an interpreter for the man who controlled our destinies.

After those "interviews" and for the next month, I rarely saw Garwood, although I knew that he was in the camp. Part of our daily routine was the arrival of Holmes with a radio, which he tuned at about four each afternoon to the broadcast of "Hanoi Hannah's" propaganda program. Every week to ten days, Garwood would appear along with Holmes. He barely spoke to us before, during, or after these broadcasts, and most of us refused to try to talk with him. Zawtocki and Pfister were exceptions because they tried to curry his favor so that they could bum tobacco from him. He always had a plentiful supply, which was further evidence to us that he enjoyed privileges that no prisoner could ever expect, and he did share the tobacco freely.

The few times that he came into our area it was usually with Holmes. However, as the weeks passed, he began to wander in alone, and when he did it was to have a confidential conversation off to the side with Grissett. Afterward, we would pump Grissett for what had been said, but he would only reply, "Nothing." We quickly suspected that Garwood was approaching his old "friend" for information about the rest of us. We had already grown cautious about Grissett anyway because he had informed on Kushner when "Doc" made a few comments about escaping. Kushner had been punished severely by the guards, and he became infuriated by the betrayal and confronted Grissett, who told him that he was sorry but that the guards "knew everything anyway, so don't tell me anything you don't want them to know because I will tell them."

Grissett had already been in captivity for nearly three years by that time, had tried unsuccessfully to escape himself, and had watched as Eisenbraun died. Under the strain of all that, he had come to believe that the Vietnamese had some special power to read his thoughts. This was our first indication that Grissett had already begun to lose his mind to the jungle and its starvation existence, a familiar psychosis every prisoner eventually would suffer to one degree or another in the months to come. So with Garwood nosing around and secretly talking with the man we believed would turn against us at the slightest possibility that he might gain his own release, we had reason enough to be wary of him.

In mid-May, Garwood called us to the cadre area for another round of individual conversations, which had some characteristics of an interrogation even if they were subtle. The questions seemed bland enough at first, but it soon became clear to us that he knew what was going on in the camp, our disputes, our bickering among ourselves, and the various states of illness among the prisoners.

Late one night at the end of May, we were in our hootch when we heard a slight rustling noise out back. We were afraid to venture outside and were very careful about how we checked out the noises for fear that it could be one of the guards. When we peeked around the corner and saw that it was Garwood, we confronted him and asked him why he was listening to us. He didn't say a word but smiled, shrugged it off, and walked away. This happened two or three other times the rest of the year, and on each of those occasions one of us would be called to the camp commander and chastised for something that he had said.

Grissett seemed to be under Garwood's influence, and that became all the more evident by June 1968. The health of the prisoners was deteriorating rapidly as a result of the slash in rations. Medicine was virtually nonexistent, and malaria and dysentery had reduced most of us to a listless misery. Then, in early June, the camp commander announced that we were to attend a political course that would help us become more "progressive."

Thoughts of Freedom

Garwood sowed the first seeds of hope in the group by telling Grissett that successful completion of the course probably would result in the release of some prisoners. Grissett was certain that this was his ticket out because he had been held longer than any of the rest of us. Although his body had been ravaged by the malnutrition, disease, and mental strain of the last three years, Grissett was still one of the toughest men I ever knew. He had sustained a remarkable level of strength for a man who had endured such hardship. Sometimes when out on food runs, Grissett would do push-ups during rest stops just to demonstrate to the Vietnamese that he was tougher than they were.

When we learned that the political course would also be accompanied by an end to the work details for gathering wood and *manioc* and an increase in our food rations, medicine, mosquito nets, and new clothing and sandals, the spirits of the entire camp lifted. But no one's rose higher than Grissett's. Buoyed by the news, he began jumping up in the morning and calling for everyone to begin our morning exercises. Most of us had neither the strength nor the will to get up, much less do calisthenics. He swept out the hootch like a whirling dervish. He did everything he could to impress the VC that he had surpassed the threshold of "progressive" and should be released, as Garwood had led him to believe he would be.

In preparation for the political course, the guards had built an open-air, thatched-roof classroom with four rows of wooden benches arranged before a head table. Propaganda posters adorned the walls: "Vietnam is one. The Vietnamese are one." "The Vietnamese will surely win; the U.S. will surely lose." "Freedom of speech is necessary in debate." The classes, we learned right away, were an intense exercise in indoctrination, including instruction in Vietnamese history and some exposure to literature. Mostly, though, everything was designed to "reeducate" the prisoners to the point that we would question why our country was in Vietnam "killing innocent women and children." During the course we were urged to write propaganda statements against the U.S. war effort.

The primary instructor was a man named Ho, who appeared to be a fairly high-ranking official with the VC. We later saw some propaganda leaflets identifying him as the equivalent of a two-star general in the National Liberation Front. His wife, he said, was a nurse at a hospital in Da Nang and was a spy for the NLF, known to us as VC. Ho ranted and cajoled in English with a strong French accent, telling us that he had taught English in Da Nang. He spoke the language fairly well, but he was one of the most thoroughly disgusting people I'd ever encountered. He swaggered, was overbearing, shrill, mean, and threatening. He always wore a camouflage green silk scarf around his neck to accent his faded, shiny blue trousers, the loose-fitting shirt commonly seen in many countries of Asia and Latin America, and his brown loafers with white socks, which he alternated with sandals from time to time. He came into the camp with an entourage of assistants, bodyguards, a camera crew, and his own cook. Among the supplies that he had his servants carry into the camp were large quantities of Ovaltine and various canned meats.

We met in the classroom at seven each morning for the course, which was scheduled to last two weeks. The morning session ended at eleven o'clock, with the afternoon session lasting from two to four. The morning session was a droning recitation from prepared documents covering four thousand years of Vietnamese history and its wars for freedom beginning with the Chinese and moving down through the ages to the current struggle against the United States.

Most of this historical instruction was basically true, but given in such excruciating detail to a group that was distrustful of the Communist version of anything, that we became bored very quickly. For the afternoon sessions, the prisoners were divided into three separate study groups led by Ho, Holmes, and Garwood. Garwood also sat at the front table during the morning portion of the class, where he was dressed as never before, or again, in fresh new silk pajamas, almost white in color, and a scarf similar to Ho's around his neck.

I didn't help matters that first day by leaving during part of Ho's oration because of a terrible spasm of diarrhea caused by a screaming case of dysentery. As often as not, I went in my pants, so I was relieved that I had even made it to the latrine in time. I had tried to catch Ho's attention to ask permission, but he was so absorbed in his talk, waving around his brown-rimmed glasses, putting them back on, and stopping for one of his many sips of Ovaltine, that he never saw me. So I quietly slipped away to take care of my business. As I returned, still tying up my pajama bottoms, Ho stopped in midsentence, and a crazed look came into his eyes. He screamed, "I can have you shot! You are trying to sabotage my course!" I raised my hand to explain my plight, but that made him even angrier. He railed on some more and then ordered me to his hootch after the morning class, where he upbraided me further and made me apologize. Then he stuck a menacing, crooked finger in my face and said, "I have heard much about you. You are very arrogant and that is a sign of a lack of discipline." That crooked finger and those wild eyes convinced me that this was a seriously deranged human being.

The afternoon sessions, with Garwood supervising one of the three groups, included the use of some Marxist indoctrination, trying to "educate" us in the evils and unfairness of life in the United States. This pitch was used persistently with the blacks, who basically made up one group. The leaders also used those sessions to tell us that the United States had broken the Geneva Convention by being in Vietnam and that we were not entitled to receive protections under the accords because we were war criminals, not prisoners of war. That was an ironic point because at all other times they reminded us that Vietnam had never signed the accords and so was not bound by them. We were told to discuss the issues that had been raised and to give "progressive" responses. We gave them answers close to what they wanted to hear but not close enough to count as voluntary propaganda that we thought they could use. When asked by the group leader why the war was illegal, immoral, and unjust, David Harker at one point said, "All wars are illegal, immoral, and unjust because innocent people are killed. Everyone should learn to live in harmony without fighting." That fell short of condemning our own country, which is prohibited by the U.S. Code of Military Conduct.

Throughout the course, Garwood remained close by Ho's side. He was dressed in full Vietnamese celebration garb and sat with the VC cadre. Probably the most dramatic instance of his participation, though, came during the brutal abuse of "Top" Williams. While Williams was answering one of Ho's questions, he committed an unpardonable error. He had used the term "ARVN." Ho flinched and then flushed. Looking first at Holmes and then at Garwood, he flew into a tirade.

"What did you say, Williams?" he bellowed. The sergeant looked surprised and then stunned and, making matters even worse, tried to explain himself.

"ARVN," he answered. "Army of the Republic of Vietnam." That sent Ho into apoplexy, and he screamed, "Puppet troops! They are nothing but puppet troops! Williams, you are trying to sabotage this course!"

Trying to Break Everyone

After a few more minutes of frenzied outbursts, Ho dismissed the class and sent us back to our hootch with orders not to talk to Williams. Soon Williams was called up to the main camp and subjected to more abuse before trying to apologize. By now the method in Ho's madness was becoming clear: He was taking a high-ranking prisoner and using him to break the entire group. We were ordered back to the classroom, where Williams was forced to apologize to us. Then we had to "criticize" him. At first, these criticisms came in the form of bland, generalized rebukes, but that did not satisfy Ho. The criticisms from the other prisoners, who were by now not only weak and sick but also straining under the emotional pressure of captivity, became harsher, in some cases almost cruel.

What followed, however, surprised all of us. Ho called on Garwood to render his criticisms. He stepped forward with venom in his eyes and in his words: "You have come to Vietnam, Williams, to commit crimes against these innocent people! I hate you, Williams, and all those like you. I spit on you, Williams!"

All of us had criticized the man, already seriously sick and weakened by the wound that was just beginning to heal, but this had been different. It was real and heartfelt. We had done it because we had to, but Garwood had done it with malice and hatred. His were the words of a fellow American, and a U.S. Marine. Williams was crushed and frightened, a different man, a broken man. He shook uncontrollably. His nose sniveled constantly. We learned only later that he had been forced at gunpoint to write a confession and then to rewrite it thirty times.

This proud, battle-tested soldier was reduced to all that he had despised as a professional. At some point during that psychological torture, his mind snapped. He told us later that he had even tried to convince Ho and Garwood that he was ready to cross over. In his enfeebled mind, he had convinced himself that he could gain the VC's confidence and then lead us all out of that camp to freedom. He had lost it, and that became obvious when Ho subjected him to more humiliation the next day, forcing Williams to express his sorrow for his unpardonable mistakes. Williams hadn't died yet, but he was as good as a dead man. His age, his wound, the jungle conditions—all of those had contributed to his decline, but Bobby Garwood delivered the blow that finally broke him. After that, it was only a matter of time.

The political course dragged on until the leaders ran out of questions, and the prisoners ran out of new answers. Ho became visibly frustrated with the lack of "progress," assuming he had any objective other than smashing the camp's morale in the first place.

That seemed to be his ulterior motive when, after the tenth or eleventh day, he declared the course over. No one, he said, would be released.

That announcement set in motion the gradual demise of Grissett, who had listened to Garwood and believed that he would be the next prisoner to receive his freedom. When Ho's announcement was made, Grissett slumped visibly on the bench where he was sitting. He sank into despair and hopelessness, abruptly ending his daily exercising and sweeping of the hootch floor to impress the guards. He just lay on the bed because he didn't care anymore. But everyone suffered. Not only were the food rations cut back to their previous levels, but the VC also began intensifying their attempts to get us to write antiwar propaganda statements. We evaded specific wording that would break any U.S. laws, but the VC were never satisfied. They began telling us that if we ever wanted to go home, and if we wanted medicine for the sick, we would have to write satisfactory statements. So we settled on a compromise in hopes that at least our names would get out, and people would know that we were alive.

Under Kushner's drafting, we submitted the statement: "We are American servicemen captured in South Vietnam. We urge American servicemen not to kill innocent women and children and for the United States to end the war soon and bring us home." We thought that was vague enough, and we signed it. Perhaps we rationalized, but ultimately we believed that the promise of medicine and other medical help for the sick and wounded was justification enough.

Then the VC changed their minds and decided that only selected prisoners would sign to make it what today would be called "politically correct." They chose Floyd Kushner as a doctor, me as a pilot, "Top" Williams, Fred Burns, and Russ Grissett as infantrymen, Denny Hammond as an Indian, and Willie Watkins as a "Negro." Only recently did I come into possession of a leaflet with a crude propaganda statement totally different from what we had written. Our signatures did not appear, but our names had been printed along with our ranks and units under text that had been written by the Vietnamese. Our long-shot hope of release, though, did not materialize, and we soon sank into a numb state of almost total demoralization.

A Horrible Skin Disease

Besides the reduction in quantity and quality of food, the supplies of medicine dwindled again. That was critical because even before Ho had arrived to conduct his political course, almost everyone in the camp started to develop a horrible skin disease. Pustules developed all over the body, including the palms of hands and soles of feet, and for several months some of the men couldn't even bend their fingers enough to grasp a spoon to feed themselves without great difficulty. The itching caused by the disease was maddening. We would lie on the hard bamboo "bed" screaming for God or someone to take us out of our misery so that the itching would stop.

Against Kushner's advice, men began to scratch and dig at their sores for relief from the itching, but that only caused them to become infected and left bloody, pus-running wounds that intensified the itching and pain. Kushner for two months had begged the

Vietnamese to provide some medicine to treat the disease. Finally, they brought him some sulfur, which they said had been removed from an undetonated U.S. bomb. The sulfur was formed into a paste, which we were told to rub all over our bodies. Within several days, the rash and boils began to recede and heal, but by then the psychological damage from such suffering—compounded by the incessant ravages of malaria, dysentery, and malnutrition—had reduced most of us to walking skeletons. Everyone had lost up to half his body weight, and had enlarged livers and spleens. Shaking chills and intermittent fevers were rampant, and lack of protein and retention of body fluid caused swelling of feet, ankles, and scrotum that made any movement terribly painful. Trying to find relief by lying down only caused swelling in the neck.

The Dying Begins

It seemed that things could not get much worse, but by September 1968, the dying began. Francis Cannon, who never fully recovered from his back wounds, had shriveled to a pitiful ninety pounds. He had been with Delta Company along with Williams, Strickland, and Harker when he was captured. No matter how hot the weather, Cannon suffered from chills and spent much of his time huddled near the cooking fire to get warm. One day, he was the only one in the hootch while the rice was cooking, and when we returned, the day's ration of food was gone. Cannon denied eating it, but we knew better.

To add to his misery, he was also a chain-smoker in a place where tobacco was scarce. We would find him sprawled under the bed searching for cigarette butts to salvage enough precious tobacco shreds to roll himself another one. Wasted finally by the harsh deprivations of the camp, he curled up motionless on the floor of the hootch by the fire pit one day in early September and lapsed into a coma. He died a few hours later and was buried in a bamboo coffin in an area just beyond the prisoner compound.

A couple of weeks later, "Top" Williams was in increasingly serious physical and mental decline after the political course. Like many of the rest of us, he had developed a serious case of edema or fluid swelling. His testicles had swollen to three times their normal size, and his legs and abdomen had also swollen to grotesque proportions, forcing fluid to press near his heart. "Doc." Kushner lacked the diuretics that the VC medics had in stock but refused to give us, or he might have saved his life.

Williams lay in his bloated state of misery while the other prisoners fed him, carried him to the latrine, and washed him. Fearful that they were about to lose another prisoner, the VC gave him a can of condensed milk. Kushner told him to dilute it so that the heavy sweetness would not exacerbate his dysentery, but Williams was in a daze. He drank it straight. Several days later, his body distended and his spirits extinguished, he began breathing sporadically and was dead within a couple of hours.

Bob Sherman, the marine who had gone off the deep end while working in the morgue stuffing body bags, never fully recovered from the month he had spent in the stocks after the April escape attempt. He shuffled around the camp disconnected from the world around him. He would sit in a spot of sunlight when one was available, but most of the time he sat inside on the sleeping pallet. We could see that he was fading and tried to get him to tell us his Marine Corps stories, or we tried to convince him to get up and move around, to take an interest in living. Once in awhile he would smile and even laugh a little, but he was really not with us. Finally, toward the end of September, he gave up, lay down, and died.

The three deaths in quick succession had a devastating psychological effect on the camp. Kushner pleaded with the VC for more and better food and more medicine to prevent further decline. He reminded the cadre that whatever value the prisoners might have to them in their beastly war strategy would be lost if they died off. Their grudging responses came too late and with too little effect. We had become desperate for some meat to eat. Garwood, in those rare, peculiar acts of kindness to us, had managed over several months to bring us six or eight eggs and one chicken that he had stolen, although he kept the drumsticks and left the remainder to feed the rest of us.

Then one night in late September, Zawtocki noticed the camp cat, which served both as a pet for the camp commander and a predator of the many rats that infested the place. After catching the cat, the men debated how to kill it. Grissett then stepped forward, took it behind the hootch, and bashed its head against a rock. While Kushner and Strickland kept watch, someone took out a rusty razor blade and skinned it. Grissett took the head and entrails and stuffed them in the latrine pit while the others boiled water to cook the cat. Within a few minutes, Kushner signaled with a low whistle that a guard was approaching. He came in, saw the cooking pot and assumed that we had caught a ferret or some other nocturnal animal, and then walked away. About ten minutes later, though, another guard came in undetected, saw the cat's severed paws on the floor, and screamed, *"Meo, meo!"* the Vietnamese word for "cat." He ran out toward the cadre sleeping area. Grissett then told everyone to admit to nothing.

Within a couple of minutes, the camp commander, Holmes, and several guards carrying kerosene lamps stormed to the hootch and ordered everyone outside. Holmes barked at Strickland, "Who killed the cat?" He said he didn't know. The questioning went down the line, with the same answer. Finally, the camp commander rattled on in Vietnamese with Holmes translating: "This was the camp commander's cat. The guards loved the cat." I thought to myself, yeah, you loved the camp dog and the camp tropical bird, but when you got hungry you killed and ate them too, didn't you? The haranguing went on for fifteen minutes with no admissions, then out of the blue, Grissett said, "I killed the cat. It was an accident. I heard a noise and threw a rock, and it killed the cat." Four or five guards pulled Grissett away from the others and kicked and beat him unmercifully.

Then Garwood stepped forward and came down the line of prisoners. He punched or elbowed Harker in the ribs, knocking him to the ground. "Someone's going to pay for letting Russ take the blame." That incident, shocking to us then, would come back more than a decade later to haunt Garwood, but at the time we saw it as just another indication of where we stood with him.

Kushner was told by a guard to remove his glasses and was slapped viciously in the face several times.

The men suspected of participating in killing the cat
were tied up and left for several hours. Then, in the
middle of the night, everyone but Grissett was untied
and told to dig a hole and bury the cat. The next
morning, one of the cadre came back and flogged
Grissett with a cane.

Another Death in Camp

That beating, combined with the despondency he suffered after the political course, drained Grissett of the
will to live, and his slow regression from that point
was irreversible. The native Texan had been a prisoner since early 1966, when he became stranded from
his patrol. He came from a troubled home and had
some minor scrapes with the law before joining the
Marine Corps. He had become a marine's marine, but
the experience of captivity had changed him and
twisted his mind. His time with Garwood and Army
Capt. Ike Eisenbraun, who had died in camp the year
before, left him confused and vulnerable. His desire
for release became an overriding passion with him,
and when that hope seemed to be beyond reach, he
could no longer cope.

He retreated into the hootch, seldom venturing out.
He had trusted Garwood before the political course
and had been betrayed. He was shocked and shattered.
Once so strong and so sure that someday he would
make it out of the jungle, he simply gave up and
began to fade away. Like many of the others—like
me—he lay on the bed and stopped eating. He refused
all prodding and encouragement. One day in late November, he curled up in a fetal position, began suck-
ing his thumb, and cried constantly for his "mama."

The day before Thanksgiving, as Kushner cradled him in his arms as he had the other three, he looked up at "Doc" and said, "Tell my mom that I love her." Then, with his dying breath, he whispered his last words, the words I will never, ever forget: "Wake me when it's over."

Just a few days later, on November 27, Bill Port became the last man in the camp to die in 1968. Port, who had lingered at the point of death since he had used his body during an NVA ambush to shield his buddies from the blast of a grenade back in January, finally could endure no longer and he expired. His gallantry and heroism, which we did not learn about until we came home, earned him a posthumous Congressional Medal of Honor. For me at the time, though, he was just another man in line ahead of me to slip mercifully into death's embrace.

8
On to Camps Three and Four

As the deaths mounted in the camp, some of us just withdrew into a shell of resignation. Others, though, like Watkins, McMillan, and Davis, managed to persevere, as did Harker and Strickland. They, too, suffered from the same diseases but seemed not to be as vulnerable to the physical or mental deterioration that left so many of us at times willing to surrender to our fates.

Both Harker and Strickland were with Delta Company when they were captured along with Williams and Cannon, and their endurance helped to sustain the group, both by the extra work they were able to do and by the example of fortitude they set. Harker, a native of Virginia, was always understanding of the sickness that others suffered and was more tolerant than some of the others when men were laid low. This was especially courageous since he suffered from a knife wound sustained during a failed escape attempt when he was first captured. The wound further weak-

ened him for the duration of his captivity, yet he refused to let it overpower his will to survive. He was
friendly and an articulate voice of reason under un-
reasonable conditions.

Strickland, from North Carolina, was cut from
much the same cloth. Like McMillan, he adapted to
the harsh conditions imposed by our captors with a
resilience common to those from rural backgrounds.
He did not react harshly to the guards but left them
well enough alone and performed the tasks demanded
of him. He exercised and kept himself as clean as
conditions would permit and avoided conflict. Even
during periods of tension among the prisoners, Strickland acted as a stabilizing force in an environment
that was inherently unstable.

Yet the deaths, once they started, also led to an
odd change in the relationships between the strong
and the weak. From March 1968 until the dying began
in September, the stress of survival had driven wedges
between us. The VC took advantage of these animos-
ities by dividing us into separate hootches, strong
with strong, weak with weak. The blacks and stronger
whites, who were resentful of the increased work they
had to do, made no secret of their feelings that we
were shirking our share of daily duties around the
camp. They constantly chided and berated us, hoping
to snap us out of our listlessness. Most of this behavior, I am sure, was motivated by their exasperation at
having to support us, and there is no escaping the
likelihood that some racial antagonism boiled to the
surface as well. But the yelling and occasional shakes
and shoves also had the effect, intended or not, of
preventing us from surrendering completely.

A Coming Together

When the men began to die in quick succession, though, the stronger prisoners began to close ranks for all of us. Their rebukes were still pointed, but they began to include an element of veiled encouragement. The blacks, especially Watkins, were always there to help a weaker man to the latrine or to clean him up if he didn't make it. They were there to help carry out Kushner's order to force-feed a man to keep him going. In a very loose way, in the face of the dying, we began to solidify as a group. As a result, I slowly began to pull out of my fatalistic resignation. I was still weak from malaria and dysentery, and the edema had caused my skin to split and ooze yellow, foul-smelling fluid, but I began trying at least to perform some limited work. I stopped sneaking and eating salt—which caused my bloated body to retain even more fluid—because I saw finally that it had helped to kill Williams. We all knew that if we didn't get our minds off dying, any one of us could be next.

Sometime in December 1968, another prisoner entered the camp. He told us his name was John Peter Johnson, a marine private. "Johnson" was somewhat of a mystery man who didn't tell us much about himself. But one day I saw that he was wearing a T-shirt with the name "Elbert" on it. He just said that his laundry had been mixed up with someone else's in his platoon before he was captured, and he avoided the issue after that.

Shortly after he came into the camp, we heard a propaganda broadcast on Holmes's radio by an American serviceman named John Peter Johnson. We turned to him and said, "Hey, John, that's you," but he vigorously denied it. For the rest of the time that he was with us in captivity, including in North Vietnam, he insisted that he was "Johnson." I learned much later that he was actually Fred Elbert—the name on the T-shirt—so future references will be to Elbert, who I believe was a strange guy, but one of us.

With Grissett buried, we hoped that the deaths would cease. The camp commander, concerned about the flurry of dying, increased the food ration somewhat. When it appeared that I was on the verge of giving up, the guards brought me a can of condensed milk to put on my rice and some bananas. We began to get a chicken once a month, or a portion of pig meat. After the diet improved, the will to survive became stronger. But it was still a struggle. The vitamin deficiency caused me to lose my night vision, and I found myself bumping into the side of the hootch or into the bamboo fence if I needed to go to the latrine pit after dark. I still was terribly weak and could walk only about twenty steps before having to stop to catch my breath and rest for five minutes. But living mattered again. We thought the dying was behind us.

Christmas, our first in captivity, was one of the few occasions when the Vietnamese showed much humanity. They gave us a banner with a star on it and allowed us to put up a small tree that we decorated with small pieces of paper. That afternoon, the radio station in Hanoi broadcast messages from several pilots about missing home and families and seeing their children grow up. Watkins was given back his New Testament by the guards and allowed to read the Christmas passages. Afterward, we said the Lord's

Prayer and sang a few carols. The camp commander told us that our celebration was because of the generous concession of humane leniency by the Vietnamese people and that if it weren't for Lyndon Johnson we all would be at home with our families.

Then he mentioned the "secret plan" of Richard M. Nixon, who had won the presidential election the month before, and he told us that he was encouraged to think that Nixon could end the war, giving us a twinkling of hope. Before the cadre left, they gave us some candy, which we divided among ourselves. Garwood had been standing there while we split the pieces up among ourselves and then rushed out. In a few minutes, the camp commander came back and told us to place all the candy in the middle of the bed until after a midnight broadcast that he wanted us to hear of U.S. pilots singing Christmas carols from their Hanoi prison. We had already heard them saying earlier in the afternoon that they had been given ham, turkey, and cranberry sauce, so we'd heard about all we wanted to hear from the prisoners in Hanoi. We told the commander that if we couldn't divvy up our Christmas candy as we chose, he could have it back or give it to Garwood, who I believe was behind the whole thing anyway. The commander relented. I guess that was as merry a Christmas as we could have had under the circumstances.

Garwood's Little Secret

It was about this time that we got some indication of where Garwood was going during his unaccompanied disappearances from the camp. We knew that he had sometimes made food runs to bring back sacks of rice and other provisions, but at other times he came back with nothing more than he had taken with him. Ike McMillan told us that he had been talking with Garwood when he had come down to the prisoners' compound one day and asked him about a satchel that he was carrying. Garwood showed him a bullhorn and told McMillan that he was going down to the plains to broadcast a message to the American soldiers at a firebase and encourage them to lay down their arms and stop fighting and killing innocent women and children.

The broadcasts were not without some risk. McMillan said Garwood mentioned that once he had sneaked up to within a couple of hundred yards from a base's perimeter to set up the battery-operated megaphone. Then he had connected the speaker to a length of commo wire that he stretched an additional two hundred yards away from the base so that if the troops on the bunker line began to shoot at the sound of his voice, he would be safely out of the line of fire. McMillan said Garwood noted that the length of commo wire wasn't quite long enough because when he began speaking, the Americans' mortars began pumping rounds out in the direction of his voice, and he was nearly hit by a couple that overshot their mark. I have no way of knowing the factual accuracy of that story, but McMillan told us that he saw the megaphone with his own eyes and that Garwood had told him all about these activities.

In early January 1969, with the slight improvements in the food, we started hoping that the morbid events of the last few months were a thing of the past. Fred Burns returned us to reality. Barely eighteen when he joined the marines at his home in Long Island, New York, Burns had been offered a scholarship to Notre Dame. Instead, he joined the corps to show his father that he was a man. He wasn't the classic, stereotypical marine: He didn't smoke, drink, or curse. He really didn't fit, but he found himself on his first patrol in Vietnam in March 1968. Somehow, he had become separated from his platoon and was quickly captured. Eventually, Bobby Garwood, a marine himself, brought him in to join us. Burns soon began wasting away like the rest of us. By Christmas of 1968, he weighed eighty pounds. Dysentery squeezed out his essence, causing him to defecate at least fifty times a day. Near the end, someone would carry him down the hill to the bamboo-slat latrine where he would stay for hours at a time. Eventually, someone would have to carry him back up. Then he would sit by the fire pit, sometimes so close that he would singe his hair or burn his skin. He didn't even notice. He didn't even care.

Kushner and others confronted him with the peril he was facing. They would implore him to try, but he couldn't try because it was too hard to make himself live anymore. Many times our Vietnamese guards would tell us that dying was easy, but living in the jungle was hard. The jungle could do horrible things to people, change them in their agony and desperation into withered hulks of desperation, bitterness, and spite. With Burns, though, it had been different. He stayed the way that he had always been—polite, gentle, grateful, and appreciative. Others had abandoned their faiths, but Burns remained a devout Catholic through it all. He prayed the rosary and gave thanks for every meager meal. On the day after New Year's Day of 1969, at age nineteen, Burns followed wherever his faith led him. All the rest of us died a little too.

Food in Sight

As the Tet lunar new year of 1969 approached, the men gazed longingly at the livestock kept by the camp cadre. Plans had been laid to try to slaughter one of the animals, preferably one of the pigs, and to make it look like an accident, but the right opportunity never presented itself. One potential target was a large sow which had made it her personal mission to help the dysentery-stricken Americans clean up their constant messes. She would invariably wander up to a man who was doing his business either at the latrine or wherever his bowels suddenly and uncontrollably released a brown ooze. The sow would be standing by to consume the smelly mess even as it hit the ground. Often a man would feel the cold, flat snout pressing into his backside while he tried to finish. After overcoming the initial disgust, we came to appreciate her help. We named her Ootsie the shit-eater.

One morning, we found Ootsie dead, her head submersed up to her neck in the latrine, suffocated in her favorite meal. The camp commander was livid at losing one of his precious animals unexpectedly. He pointed at Kushner and then at the dead sow, apparently gesturing for him to bring the sow back to life. Kushner was furious. When his own men were dying in his arms he had not been allowed to practice his medicine. Now they expected him to revive a dead pig. Kushner held his temper and then calmly told the interpreter to tell the commander to give the sow mouth-to-mouth resuscitation. Fortunately for all of us, the words must have gotten lost in translation, because the officer just nodded his head and walked away. Later, Ootsie was butchered. The camp staff ate the meat. The prisoners' portion was, predictably, the head. We ate every morsel of meat we could scrape from her skull.

Chickens also became more abundant early in 1969. As the guards' flock grew, they paid less and less attention to the birds while we paid more and more attention. Eventually, the guards began to give us a few chicks of our own to raise. Then we acquired a rooster we named Snoopy. When the bird got big enough, we took a vote. We had become attached to our pet rooster, but the vote was unanimous. Snoopy went into the pot. Soon, the guards had to contend with a "weasel" that was eating their chickens. They never could quite understand why the weasel killed only their chickens and never ours. Efforts to catch the predator failed, and it was a good thing because the weasel had two legs. With Ike McMillan as our chief chicken-snatcher, we could grab, kill, and boil a chicken in almost no time at all.

The next couple of months in 1969 were routine. In late January, though, we had noticed that the VC were working on some kind of project at the base of the hill. At first we thought it was probably a special hootch for a high-ranking officer because the cadre was taking plenty of good food down to it. Someone asked Garwood what was going on, and he said that an American defector had slipped away from a firebase, turned himself over to the NLF, and was writing antiwar messages before being moved for reeducation in the north. But within a few days, the guards brought him up and put him in with us. He was Gus

Mehrer, a real hippie. He was a draftee, and to say the least, his heart wasn't in the war effort. He had drawn peace symbols on his army fatigue shirt and told us he'd had it with his lieutenant because he wouldn't let him smoke dope. So he just walked away and was captured on Christmas Day, 1968. He told us that he never really had any intention of crossing over, but he mentioned on a few occasions something vague about "torture" during his early captivity. We never could be sure whether he meant physical brutality or psychological coercion because he showed no signs of having been beaten.

At any rate, he decided to make the best of a bad situation and began telling the VC whatever they wanted to hear for awhile. When he started to give the impression that he was ready to cross over, that was when the guards gave him special treatment in the form of bananas, tobacco, and sugar. Garwood had even worked with him, encouraging him to join him in his "work," but it became clear that Mehrer really wasn't on anybody's side in the war but Mehrer's. Finally, he refused to cooperate anymore, his favorable treatment stopped, and he was sent to join the rest of us in the compound. Mehrer always insisted that he had at no time crossed over to the VC. He seemed a little flaky to me, but he was an agreeable enough guy, and we all got along with him pretty well. He remained relatively strong all during the time in the jungle and was able to be a great help on the food runs.

Increased Bombing Activity

By the end of February 1969, U.S. air activity began to intensify in the area. Some of the bombing runs

Here I am in Saigon. This was one of the last photographs taken of me before I became a POW.

When I was commissioned as a WO-1 at Fort Rucker, my father, then a lieutenant colonel, pinned on my bars.

This is the scene of my crash as it appeared on January 7, two mornings after the crash. The crew is no longer here. Carson is in the process of making his escape, and Pfister, Lewis, and I have already completed the first day of our five years as POWs. Legend: A—My chopper, barely identifiable from this distance. B—the "river" (really just a creek) which Carson crawled into to escape. C—Sixteen NVA antiaircraft guns were hidden in these trees. They shot me down and, with the help of bad weather, prevented my rescue in spite of daring attempts. D—In this area, an infantry unit had been overrun. I was shot down trying to help them. Four different medevac helicopters attempted to haul out wounded the morning of January 6, but only one made it. The pilot, Major Brady, was awarded the Congressional Medal of Honor for flying four trips into the antiaircraft fire and hauling out thirty-nine wounded.

After leaving Vietnam, we landed at Clark Air Force Base in the Philippines and spent three days at the hospital there. This group photo includes most of the POWs who were captured and held in the jungles of South Vietnam. I'm at the very back, in the middle.

This is the group of friends who were waiting for me at McGuire.

From Clark, I flew to McGuire Air Force Base in New Jersey. Here I'm taking my first steps on U.S. soil and have broken ranks to meet a group of friends who came to welcome me home.

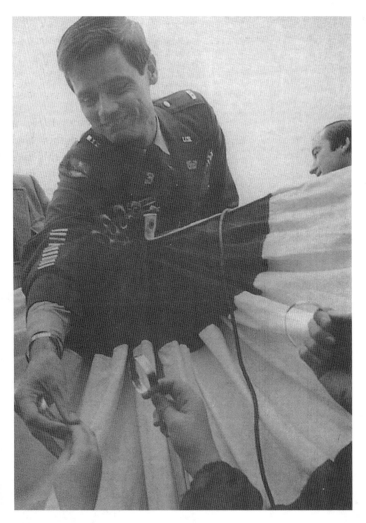

During the parade ceremony, people came up to me and gave me the Frank Anton POW bracelets they'd been wearing. I still have hundreds of them.

LEFT TO RIGHT: Me, Robert Lewis (my crewchief and fellow POW), and Chuck Carlock. We're at the Firebirds reunion in May 1995. (CATHY CARLOCK)

were carried out by fighters, but the heaviest patterns were coming from the B-52s flying high beyond ear-shot. One day, while I was playing cards with Mc-Millan and Davis, one bomb fell no more than three hundred yards from the camp. I had just touched my foot to the floor to begin shuffling toward the bomb shelter as fast as I could, which was not very fast, when McMillan and Davis both bolted right over me, knocking me over and running right through the thatched wall of the hootch to the shelter. It's a good thing that no other bombs were on their way into the compound, but that one apparently was close enough to convince the Vietnamese that it was time to move. Within a couple of weeks, we packed up and walked the six hours to Camp Three.

This camp was similar to the others, built on a hillside near a ridgeline and covered by triple-canopy jungle, but it was larger than Camp Two. Its best fea-ture from the prisoners' perspective was the fast-running stream with a far superior bathing pool than the previous two camps. Above the camp, on top of the ridge, was a cucumber field, which for awhile provided a source of vegetables that enriched our di-ets, although we eventually got pretty sick of cucum-bers. Later in the year, however, U.S. aircraft began spraying defoliant on the field, and that was almost the end of that—but not before the guards made us pick all the remaining contaminated cucumbers and eat them all until they were gone. To my knowledge, no one suffered any complications from the defoliant because we thoroughly scrubbed them with water.

Life in Camp Three soon settled into a pretty un-eventful routine. We still had to gather wood for the camp and dig *manioc* to supplement our rice, but the

Sketch of Viet Cong POW Camp Drawn by Frank Anton during his Debrief after Release

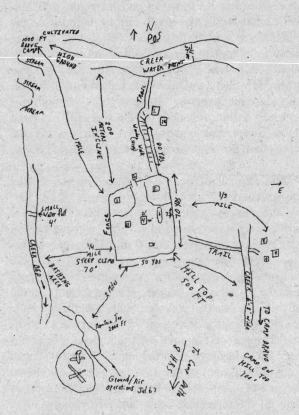

1 VC Kitchen

2 Guard

3 ARVN POWs

4 US POWs

5 German POWs

6 Bomb Shelter (Underground)

7 German Graves

8 Latrine

9 Mountain People Village

10 VC Billets

11 Unknown Building

generally improved diets helped bring the worst aspects of our various diseases under some control. One element of jungle life, though, never left us—rats. They weren't like the sewer rats I remember seeing when I was growing up in Philly. They seemed more tame and, I had hoped, not as likely to carry diseases like the city rats did. But they were awfully clever. No matter where the men tried to hide their food or put it out of reach, the rats would get it. One of us had placed a fist-sized ball of cooked rice in a piece of torn shirt, tied it with a piece of string, and suspended it from the roof of the hootch. The string hung down about eight feet from the ceiling cross-support, but during the night a rat somehow climbed down the string, gnawed away the cloth, and ate every last kernel of the rice.

They were everywhere, and except for occasionally catching and eating them, we managed to ignore them. One night I was awakened on the bed by something tickling my foot. I looked down and saw a small rat chewing on my toe. I kicked him off and went back to sleep. Some things we just had to get used to.

Soon after we had set up in the new camp, another American prisoner joined us. Coy Tinsley was captured in March 1969, and with the addition of Elbert and Mehrer, our number had increased to seventeen. But Tinsley turned out to be lucky. He was a short-timer by the time he arrived and didn't even know it. He immediately got pretty sick, and the VC medics brought in medicines that they administered through an intravenous unit. "Doc" Kushner was outraged. If he had had such equipment in Camp Two, he felt that he could have saved several lives. He was angry and bitter that the Vietnamese had withheld such equipment back then.

As it was, he was reduced to providing on the sly what basic care he could for the men when they needed it. For Julius Long, that was a lifesaver. He'd come close enough to being killed when his Americal Division unit had been overrun in May 1968, and the ARVNs his company was moving in to relieve had turned and began fighting with the NVA. Long took cover from the American artillery barrage in a dirt and log blockhouse to await his rescue. A Firebird gunship was shot down, and the slick that was to pull out Long diverted to pick up the downed gunship crew. That night an NVA search patrol tried to force Long out of his shelter, but he killed several of them when they tried to enter the tiny entrance, so they withdrew. When he felt that the coast was clear, he began walking along a road and hailed an oncoming U.S. jeep. Unfortunately, the vehicle had been captured by a VC squad, and Long fell into their hands before he could escape again. Once in camp with us, the West Virginia native became ill with malaria and dysentery and was in serious mental decline as well. He and I sat on the bamboo bed for days at a time, brooding under his poncho liner, coming out only for meals.

About a year after he joined us, Long one day collapsed, ashen-faced and short of breath. Kushner diagnosed the condition as a heart attack, and he began pounding on his chest. In the process he cracked a couple of ribs, but without his medical expertise, which the Vietnamese had denied to so many others, Long never would have survived that experience, much less four more years of captivity.

Women in Camp

In late June 1969, four new faces showed up in camp—Caucasians, two men and two women. We were beside ourselves at seeing white females, and it seemed almost like a vision. Everyone was so shocked that we were stunned into silent awe. Monika Schwinn, Hindrika Kortmann, Bernhard Diehl, and Georg Bartsh were German nurses who had come to Vietnam to perform humanitarian work in a hospital at Anh Hoa, near Da Nang. They had taken a drive to a village near Anh Hoa in late April and had been abducted by the VC. Walked from place to place for nearly three months, the nurses appeared to be in reasonably good condition considering their plight. They clearly were international noncombatants and appeared to be victims of a terrible mistake, but the Vietnamese proved impervious to making amends for such "mistakes."

Actually, only three came in that first day, the two men and Hindrika Kortmann, who was nicknamed Rika. Monika Schwinn had stayed back on the trail with Marie-Luise Kerber, who had become sick. By the time Monika came a few days later, she told the others that Marie-Luise had died suddenly on the trail of complications from malaria. Bernhard and Georg seemed to be almost stoic in hearing the news, but Rika was obviously distraught. Monika put her arm around her to comfort her. Right away, some of the American prisoners were told to go into the forest to cut wood for a new hootch. Within a matter of three or four days, the Vietnamese guards had fashioned a new hootch not far from ours. Throughout the time that the Germans were in the camp, we were ordered not to talk with them, although we managed to have a few brief conversations when the guards weren't looking.

The VC treated them fairly generously, giving them more food than they could actually eat. When they were able, one of the Germans would put some of their extra food in a leather shaving kit and slip it through the bamboo fence to us. We helped wash their clothes at the stream, but there were very few chances to establish any kind of relationship with them, first because the guards prevented us from doing so and also because most of them spoke only spotty English, and none of us spoke German.

One day, while Rika was washing down at the stream, Garwood slipped quietly up near her. She was quite pretty and had an attractive figure. But when Garwood touched her hand, she was very frightened and returned to her hootch. From that day on, we seldom saw her at all. Then, in late September or early October, Rika was stricken with some illness, declined very rapidly, and died suddenly. Almost as if in a sympathetic reaction, Georg became sick and also died quickly. The American prisoners dug the graves for the two just behind the prisoners' compound. Mehrer wove a little wreath of flowers that he gave to Kushner, who spoke a few words in a brief funeral ceremony and then placed the wreath between the graves. Afterward, we could tell that Monika and Bernhard were distraught and afraid. Then they disappeared. We had no idea what happened to them but learned several years later that the two had been taken to Hanoi. They remained in captivity until Operation

Homecoming in 1973, most of their time spent confined in isolation in a Hanoi prison.

Garwood in Mourning

Not long after Monika and Bernhard left, Ho Chi Minh died. All the Vietnamese, of course, were in deep mourning. Garwood brought us the news, and he came wearing a black armband just like the one worn by the other guards. He told us grimly that we were to be quiet, that we were not to make any fuss or laugh because that would make the Vietnamese extremely angry. For several days, whenever we saw him, Garwood's eyes were red and teary just like the camp guards and cadre. He had succeeded in impressing us with the importance of "behaving" because there was no doubt in our minds that he meant what he had said.

By the end of October, the VC had learned of a giant antiwar march scheduled in November 1969 in Washington, D.C. So, unknown to us, they began planning a prisoner release in hopes of gaining some political advantage from the coinciding events. All of us were interviewed by the camp commander with Garwood interpreting. My interview lasted only a few moments. When asked what I would do if released, my answer was simple: "I'd come back and bomb you some more." Garwood looked at me, and in the only act of generosity he ever made to me personally, he asked, "Do you want me to tell him that?" I said nothing, and he did not translate my comment.

After all the interviews, the camp cadre conferred with the commander, and they finally decided to begin a special indoctrination course for Watkins and

Strickland. It was strictly secret; they weren't supposed to tell the rest of us that they had been chosen for release. Both had been among the strongest prisoners to endure the terrible conditions in Camp Two, and we knew that they were not "progressive" by any Vietnamese definition. Without the pushing from Watkins, many of us would not have survived. Strickland also worked hard to keep the VC guards off our backs. And neither one of them had really participated in writing any of the statements the prisoners gave to the Vietnamese because Kushner and I did most of the drafting. But the fact that they were reasonably healthy at the time made them much more presentable prisoners for the "lenient and humane" Vietnamese to release. And as a black and a white, they also provided a politically appealing combination.

We thought that maybe Zawtocki would be another likely candidate. He had been as close to a friend for Garwood as anyone in the camp. The two had even traded rings a few months before, although Zawtocki said that he had lost Garwood's. Instead, the cadre tapped Coy Tinsley, the tall, strapping young army enlisted man from Tennessee who joined us in March 1969. He had contracted serum hepatitis—at least that's what Kushner told them—and the last thing the VC wanted was another death on their hands, or at least a serious infectious disease that could threaten them as much as the prisoners. So they decided to get rid of Tinsley.

When we learned of the impending releases, each remaining man naturally was disappointed at first that he wasn't selected, but then we grew hopeful that perhaps more would be freed soon. At the very least, we knew that a great banquet lay ahead of us. We always expected as much on such occasions. In fact there were two feasts this time. For the first, none of the high-ranking VC officers was present to deliver the usual ceremonial speeches, although we gorged ourselves as Grissett had once taught us to do. Not satisfied, camp staff held the second banquet with a repeat of the meal and an emphasis on obligatory political speeches before Watkins, Strickland, and Tinsley were adorned in their white pajamas and red sashes and bid good-bye.

During their final indoctrination sessions, they were asked if they would go to the antiwar rally in Washington the next month and deliver stirring speeches about the evils of the U.S. war criminals who were killing Vietnamese innocents. Naturally, they all agreed to go and deliver the message. Years later, all three admitted that they never made it to Washington.

And Garwood, Too

On the same day that Watkins, Strickland, and Tinsley left the camp on their walk to freedom, Bobby Garwood also disappeared. We never saw him in Vietnam again, but several of us did see him ten years later—in America.

As with the last prisoner release, we realized that we would have to move again soon. But the VC this time were not in a big hurry for some reason, and more than a month went by before we began making preparations. Finally, the word came down the week before Christmas 1969, and we set off toward Camp Four. Unfortunately, by then Zawtocki had obviously begun to lose heart. Whether Garwood's departure had anything to do with it I don't know. He may have been hoping to be in Tinsley's place, but whatever was eating at him, it took him down. By the time we moved out during a driving rain, he had already stopped eating completely. He was so weak on the trail during our march to the new camp that he finally collapsed. The guards carried him to a Montagnard village about a mile or two from our destination and left him with a blanket so that he could rest and try to recover some strength.

Harker and Davis were sent with a couple of guards the next morning to retrieve him, and they found Zawtocki huddled motionless next to a fire, wrapped in the blanket. He was staring emptily into space, a look we had seen all too many times. Harker and Davis tried to bring him back to reality, telling him to think about his parents and his sisters back in New York, how he was the only son and had to carry on the family name. They also reminded him that Watkins and Strickland were going to tell his folks that he was alive and that he didn't want to die. "No, I don't want to," he told them, "but it's so hard." After he promised that he would try to eat, they went back to camp.

Late Christmas Eve, someone came into the hootch and said that Zawtocki had died, making for a very gloomy Christmas that year. There were no fervent political speeches, no readings from the departed Watkins's New Testament, no candy. We had been given a can of condensed milk and heated water so we could dilute it and give everyone an equal portion. Then in subdued voices we sang a few carols, drank the warm, watered-down milk, and went to bed.

The guards brought Zawtocki's body from the vil-

Sketch of POW Camp drawn by Frank Anton during his Debrief after Release

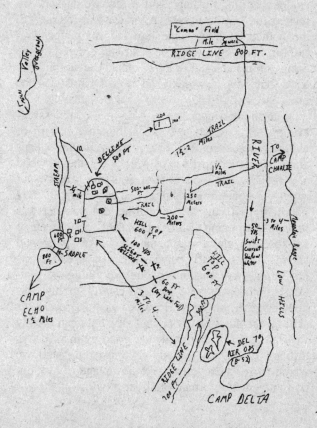

1 Vegetable Garden
2 Cadre Kitchen
3 VC Cadre Billets
4 US POWs
5 ARVN POWs
6 Corn and Comeo Field
7 Guard
8 VC Guard Huts
9 Graves
10 Water line (Bamboo Trench)

lage, and on Christmas Day we dug a shallow grave in the hard, rocky ground and laid him to rest in a bamboo coffin. Kushner said a few words, and we recited the Lord's Prayer. After we had returned to the hootch, Holmes came into the compound with tears in his eyes. He had been strictly ordered by the camp commander not to let Zawtocki die, he said bitterly, but now Zawtocki had ruined Christmas for everyone.

With the dawning of a new decade, countless uneventful days began to run together in a pattern of almost bearable routine. The guards generally left us alone except to supervise us while we gathered wood and *manioc*. The food, at least, was in a little greater supply, although it was still as bad as always. In early February 1970, the last new American prisoner was brought into camp, which accounted for thirteen of us. Jose Anzuldua was a marine linguist who had attended the military language school at Monterey, California. Anzuldua understood everything the Vietnamese said, but he was very careful to hide his knowledge from them. He was able to conceal his skill for the duration of our captivity, but I can't really say that it did us any particular good by then. It was difficult to do any serious eavesdropping, and we weren't strong enough to take advantage of any opportunity such information might provide.

Another Death in Camp

By early 1970, we felt that at least the deaths among us had come to an end. But we were wrong. Denny Hammond, one of the five men Garwood had herded into Camp Two in March 1968, came down with a terrible case of dysentery. Many of the other prisoners had trouble working up much sympathy for him because he had such a harsh mean streak. When others during the frightful period of 1968 had been fouling themselves with uncontrollable diarrhea, Hammond had complained loudly about their stinking messes. Now it was his turn, and he was too weak to move himself to the latrine. He just lay on the bed as so many of us had done during the worst of the sickness the year before. We would urge him to try to get up to go outside, hoping to get him to take control of the life that was slipping away from him.

One day I sat with him in a spot of rare sunlight that pierced through the jungle canopy, and he must have known that he was dying. His body had all but shut down from the diarrhea, and he was fading fast. He turned to me, looked straight into my eyes and asked me to do him two favors. The first was to tell his mom and dad what had happened to him. The other was: "Make sure you get Garwood." Hammond was proud to be a marine, and he was especially bitter about Garwood. I told him, sure, I would tell his folks all about him when I got home, and then I reminded him that I had already told Garwood not to come home.

On March 17, 1970, curled up on his bed and wasted away, Hammond died. We buried him down the hill next to Zawtocki. Now we had been reduced to an even dozen, but that finally was the end of the dying.

As spring advanced into summer, the night artillery fire and aerial bombing began to increase in the vicinity of the camp. We had come to believe that none of our camps had ever been hit directly because the

Americans knew where we were and fired either short or long, or to the left or right of the camp during their fire missions. One night in July 1970, though, we heard a heavy series of explosions "walking" in our direction. Most of us moved toward the bomb shelter, but Mehrer, for some reason, ignored the incoming blasts and stood fast. Then a shell hit in the trees just beyond our hootch with a deafening roar, and he finally came flying into the shelter, scared to death.

One afternoon about this time, McMillan and I were collecting firewood beyond the compound. By then, the guards didn't seem to worry about our trying to escape, and no one was sent to watch us. We had strayed farther and farther away, foraging for some peppers to spice up our bland rice. We couldn't have heard the B-52s flying high overhead because of their altitude, but we also were oblivious because we were so intent on finding some precious peppers. But a B-52 strike, if it didn't kill a person outright, was such an awesome force that it could literally cause that person to lose his mind. Many a time we had heard the grunts tell of sweeping an area after the huge planes had administered a lethal pounding and finding enemy soldiers wandering aimlessly, reduced to helpless zombies by the shock of the concussions. Even their underground shelters had been no refuge.

Suddenly our focus on firewood and peppers was shattered by explosions as they reverberated in the adjoining valley several miles away. Because of our weakened physical condition, we were slow to react to the imminent danger. Granted, we were somewhat disconcerted, but we weren't alarmed enough to begin running in the opposite direction. In a matter of a minute or so, a second load of bombs blasted into the jungle just a mile away and continued on a direct line toward where we were standing. Before we could react, a third salvo shook the ground with such roaring, blasting force a few hundred yards away that we were knocked to our hands and knees and engulfed in a swirl of dirt, smoke, and visible shock waves. We now were properly terrified. A fourth rack of bombs should have fallen directly on us, blowing our skinny asses to shreds.

We already had lost our minds, at least temporarily. In a truly absurd effort to take cover, McMillan grabbed a tiny bamboo tree. He squatted down behind that two-inch-thick stick of "protection" to hide himself from the deadly hit we knew was about to fall on us. In an act of further lunacy, I latched onto McMillan from behind. I crouched down to make myself as small as possible. Then McMillan spun around quickly and jumped behind me as I crept forward to hunker behind the "cover" of the bamboo. When I felt him behind me, I whirled around and grabbed him from behind once again. We both waddled up in a crouch to shield ourselves from the coming blast of fire and steel, glued together by raw fear.

The entire scene could have been from Laurel and Hardy or the Keystone Kops! For those few terrifying minutes, though, our action made perfect sense to two men bent on self-preservation. We cowered in dread, waiting for the shrill whistle of the bombs, but silence had fallen on the macabre scene. We waited to die, but nothing happened. It was over. Slowly we separated ourselves from each other and started to laugh. We laughed so hard that we fell on the ground, rolling around in joyous release until tears flowed down our faces. We hugged each other, jumped around, and pointed at "our" tree that had "shielded" us. For a few fleeting moments, we forgot our status in a life that at once was so precious.

For the rest of 1970, the shelling continued, but the camp never was so threatened again by direct hits. Our guards were afraid, however, that the American bombers might have detected their location. Two or three times in the late fall, they moved us to another camp temporarily as a precaution. The new camp had a huge rock outcropping, forming an open cave in the jungle that served as a natural bomb shelter. We would spend a week or so under the protective cover of the rock and then move back into Camp Four.

Sometime in early January 1971, the guards began making references to "the north." It wasn't the first time. They had mentioned several times after we got to Camp Four that at some point we would be going to Hanoi, but they were never specific. The air attacks and artillery apparently were starting to make our area too hot for their comfort, and they certainly weren't doing much for our mental health either. Just as the VC finally were providing some canned food to supplement our diets, and some color was finally beginning to come into our sallow skin, we began to fear that our own jets and artillery were going to finish the job that jungle captivity had started.

The B-52 attacks had begun to escalate in early 1971, and howitzers were pouring shells into the hills not far from us. A few rounds came close enough to send hot, jagged shrapnel screaming over our heads and shearing off limbs of trees nearby.

Getting Ready to March

Our first indication that there was some kind of plan in the works to move came in early 1971. I was still the weakest man among the twelve of us and the one most likely to hold up our progress along the trail. So in obvious preparation, the guards began making me walk down the hill to the stream every day carrying a pack loaded with rocks. A guard could make the trip down the 250-yard trail and back to the top in about five minutes. The other prisoners could make the trek in about fifteen minutes, but I was in such bad shape that I took more than an hour.

The guards apparently thought that I was not a threat to escape, so they sent me to do my "training" alone. One day, I said to hell with it and took the rocks out of the pack and threw them on the ground. I made the long walk down and back up, put the rocks back in the pack and reported back to the camp. My conditioning program might not have been going according to plan, but my weary, blurred mind was conjuring up a reverie so real to me that I began to expect to reach the bottom of the long trail and find American rescuers waiting to take me home. They were never there, of course.

On a clear, early afternoon around February 1, 1971, I was sitting alone at the far end of the compound. The other prisoners were either lying on the bed or lounging idly by the hootch. That was when I heard it, the low-droning of helicopters approaching in the distance. I struggled to my feet, straining to hear. I was sure of it. "Choppers, guys! I hear chop-

Sketch of POW Camp drawn by Frank Anton during his Debrief after Release

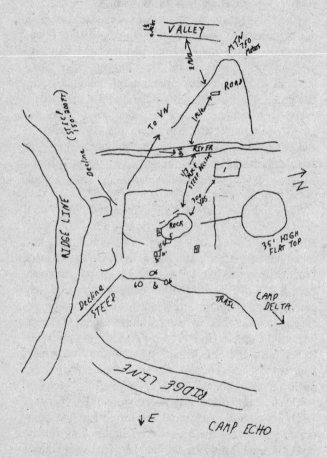

1 Open Field (Corn and Sugar Cane)   4 VC Billets
2 ARVN POWs Lean-to   5 Bomb Shelter (Under Rock)
3 US POWs   6 Rocks

pers and lots of them!" The others looked at me curiously as if I were addled and then ignored me. Then they heard it, too, and so did the guards.

A swarm of Huey slicks and gunships, three big, lumbering Chinooks, a white medivac ship, Cobra gunships, and observation choppers circled overhead and then began spiraling downward toward the camp. As they descended, one of the guards aimed his rifle upward and drew a bead, but another grabbed the barrel and yelled something at him in Vietnamese. I guessed that he was telling him not to give away our exact location because the jungle would camouflage us for a few more minutes. As the formation came nearer, the guards rushed toward us and ordered us to climb into the bomb shelter. I was the first one shoved into the hole. Then the VC changed their minds and decided to make a run for it rather than get trapped in a firefight if those Chinooks were carrying a couple of companies of infantry.

The guards began grabbing prisoners and pulling them back out of the shelter. I hoped that in the confusion they would forget about me and leave me behind, but a guard poked his head into the shelter and pointed his bayonet at me and yelled, *"Di di!"*—move! I crawled out, and before my eyes was the OH-58 hovering less than forty feet above the prisoners' hootch, its skids almost touching the roof. The pilot had tossed a red smoke grenade into the guards' pigpen. The face of an American infantry captain was looking right at me from the 'copter, and I froze where I was standing. Then, as my eyes stared right into that captain's eyes, the guard poked me in the back with his bayonet and yelled again, *"Di di mau!"*

He shoved me in the direction of the trail into the jungle. The roar of the rotor blades receded as we scurried into the dense trees. No one but the guard followed me.

9
March to Hanoi

Within a day or two after the attempted rescue at Camp Four, after we had spent the night in the jungle to avoid being trapped in a possible American assault on the camp, the guards brought us back and assembled us for a meeting. They asked what would make us most happy, and naturally our answer was to be released. They said, "No, you're going to Hanoi." The next day, they divided us into two groups of six each. Floyd Kushner, Julius Long, David Harker, Fred Elbert, Jim Pfister, and I were in the first group. The four blacks, James Daly, Ike McMillan, Tom Davis, and Robert Lewis were joined by Gus Mehrer, who claimed to be part Indian, and Jose Anzuldua, who was Mexican-American.

We never really understood why they broke us down racially, but that seemed to be one of their constant tactics all the time we were held prisoner in the south. The Vietnamese told us that we would walk for ten days to Laos. They issued us hammocks, a plastic sheet for a ground cover, a can of milk, a can of mackerel, a ten-day ration of rice, and a backpack made from a wheat sack with cloth straps sewn onto the back. We were told that the food and supplies were only for the first ten days because after that we would be staying in what they called socialist "liberation" camps along the way.

My group was the first to leave. The others would follow in ten days. I presume this tactic was designed to keep from losing all the prisoners in one attack if we got caught in an air strike or maybe an American ambush, which wasn't likely that far west and close to the Laotian border. For the first few days, we traveled through jungle trails across steep hills that were almost mountains. We had to ford two or three rivers with extremely swift currents and deep eddies. Picking our way across the big rocks poking out of the torrents was treacherous, and our footing was precarious on the wet, slippery surfaces. Being as weak as we were, the trek was all the more perilous. We were in constant fear of falling in and drowning.

Painful Steps, Falling Behind

After four or five days, Kushner and I began falling behind a little more each day. The edema in my feet, ankles, legs, and scrotum had worsened each day, the fluid swelling my lower extremities into huge, puffy masses. The skin on my feet, which would depress more than two inches at the touch and leave an imprint that would last for two or three minutes, began to split. Each step brought a shooting, searing pain that made my progress very slow. At most, I would walk a hundred yards before stopping in agony. I began yelling at the guards, "Kill me!" Kushner was having the same problem.

At first, the guards had let the others wait for us to catch up, but then Kushner and I would fall behind again. Before long, even the two of us would get separated, and we would arrive at the camp hours after the others. It was the rainy season, and we were constantly soaked to the bone and chilled. After trudging through low, muddy areas we would emerge to find dozens of huge leeches four to five inches long attached to us. They were so big that they were hard to get off, and the places on our skin where they attached themselves were scarred forever.

On the eighth or ninth day, our group reached what appeared to be a hospital, a bamboo structure built in the heavy foliage and well camouflaged. Long had twisted his ankle badly on the trail and was having great difficulty in walking. By then, Kushner seemed to have improved somehow, at least enough that he was able to keep up with the rest of the group. I seemed to be getting only worse. I could barely lift my feet off the ground, each step being agonizingly painful. The pack, as light as it was, seemed heavy beyond bearing. Others were covering distances in seven or eight hours that took me ten or twelve.

The guards chattered among themselves for a minute or two after we came up to the jungle hospital then decided that Long and I would stay behind while the others went on. We remained there for twelve days, mostly just lying in hammocks all day. The medics served us much more rice than we had been eating on the trail, and the variety of food was much better. There was nothing for us to do but lie around and talk, mostly about food and the hope that maybe things would change for the better in the north. We listened to some propaganda broadcasts by American pilots in Hanoi who told how they had received ham and other good food for Christmas. We talked ourselves into thinking things really were going to be better for us up there. Eventually, however, we would learn that the broadcasts were essentially a cruel hoax, but for the time being we were encouraged by them.

After twelve days, the other group caught up with us, so we went on with them. When we got to the end of the scheduled ten-day march, the guards put us on a truck and told us that we were in Laos. This was as close to civilization as we had been in three years, and while we lumbered along in the luxury of the blue Russian-made truck we broke into a rendition of "Where Have All the Flowers Gone?" But we hadn't finished the first verse when one of the guards told us to keep quiet.

Looking through the wooden sideboards of the truck bed, I was shocked to see crews with trucks and a bulldozer rapidly repairing craters blown in the trail by bombs. As we passed, we looked on with some awe at the persistence and ingenuity of the Vietnamese who somehow kept that road open so that they could keep fighting the war. No sooner had the bombs torn it up than they were back at work repairing the damage. A hundred Vietnamese with homemade shovels would appear from nowhere, working hurriedly to make the road serviceable.

We were on the Ho Chi Minh trail, a hard-packed surface of dirt and grass that cut through the jungle roughly five hundred miles along the Laos-Vietnam border just inside Laos. Some areas were in the open, others were camouflaged with trees and vines where the road disappeared into the jungle, virtually cutting a tunnel through long sections of triple-canopy forest. We rode through several such sections for the rest of that day, stopping at guard checkpoints every so often, and then we were told to climb down and begin walking again. That was the last riding we did until we arrived in North Vietnam.

As we walked along the trail, we were always in the company of large groups of people, at least one hundred and at times as many as three hundred, each accompanied by a guard or leader who carried the ticket of passage for the group. The leaders were taking constant head counts to make certain that only authorized people were in their appointed groups. Many of the travelers were women and children, some of whom were wounded, and were moving north from as far away as Saigon. Our guards would blend us in with them. Because many sections of the trail were in the open, the herd strategy began to make sense when we would look up and see the silver glint of American fighter planes in the sky. As far as the pilots could tell, these masses of humanity were just innocent civilians or refugees going about their business.

We would walk along with these large groups and stop for the night at "liberation" camps which were situated at intervals of about a five-hour walk, all connected by field telephones. I began calling them "pony express stations" because they were located every few miles on the edge of the trail. Each stop had several bamboo hootches, a kitchen, mess hall, and bathing areas at rivers or streams. At every camp, travelers were checked by a commander against a roster and assigned to a hootch, which usually was dug about five feet into the ground for protection against air strikes. We would string our hammocks between posts driven into the earth floor. If the hootches were full, we slept outside in the night chill. At the end of each hootch was an underground bomb shelter, reinforced by logs. The mess halls served plenty of rice, vegetables, and meat almost every day, and the prisoners—identified by the guards as "progressive" Americans to avoid violent retaliation from others traveling in the group—always got served first.

At some of the stations, civilian travelers would upbraid the station commander for conditions that they thought were unsatisfactory. For the first ten days or so I actually felt as if I might start feeling decent again. The guards took us at a leisurely pace, probably because the longer they could stretch out such a cush job with plenty of food, the longer they could avoid having to go back to the war.

The Enemy Up Close

We would get up early each morning, eat breakfast, fill canteens, and gather for an assembly where the commander would brief the group on what to expect on the next part of the trail, whether air strikes from enemy planes might be likely, and what evasive measures to take. Back on the trail, we often passed large units of NVA soldiers heading south and carrying rockets and other heavy weapons. Usually they were marching in a relaxed formation, but occasionally a convoy of trucks loaded with soldiers would rumble by, forcing us to the side of the trail until they had passed.

At one point, just before one of our guards motioned us off the trail toward a small clearing where we could take a rest break, a group of fifty women NVA soldiers coming from the opposite direction rounded a bend in the trail. When they saw us, they squealed, *"My, my!"*—Americans!—and all ran into the jungle. I puzzled over such a bizarre reaction from "liberation fighters" and wished that their brothers-in-arms had reacted the same way while I was lying in that rice paddy more than three years before.

Then the swelling came back to my feet, ankles, and legs, and instead of trying to walk to every other station in a day, we only made it to the next one and stopped for the night to rest. Some of the heartier prisoners thought that I was intentionally slowing them down and complained, but after fifteen days in Laos I began falling behind again. Finally, screaming from the pain, I couldn't go on. Two guards placed me in a hammock and took me to the nearest hospital, which was only a couple of miles away, while the others pushed ahead.

When I got to the hospital, Fred Elbert was already there. He had been with the first group of prisoners that I had been with before I fell out the first time, and he had come down with a serious case of malaria. For the month that we stayed there, we were treated very well, with plenty of food and rest. Even though the large bamboo structure was fairly close to the trail and built right out in the open, American planes never bombed it, we were told, because our pilots knew that it was a hospital, which helped us to relax all the more for our recuperation.

This unexpected respite in our march gave us a great deal of time to talk and get better acquainted. At the time, I still thought his name was John Peter Johnson, and he never let us know much about himself. But I grilled him so long that I finally learned his real identity. I kept reminding him that we had seen the name "Elbert" on his T-shirt the first day he came into camp. He never admitted in so many words what his real name was, but when I pressed him he just looked at me and chuckled about the confusion. He still went by "Johnson" until we had been in Hanoi for some time.

When our month of recuperation in the hospital was over, one of the two guards who had been left with us got sick—although I was never sure he really was. We extended our stay for another three weeks, which gave us even more rest and the chance to build up our strength. We were going to need it. The two groups of men who had already gone ahead of us arrived in Hanoi sometime in early April after a two-month walk. Elbert and I were not to get there until August—a full six months after starting out—because of his malaria and the persistent problems I was having. Not only was I afflicted with the edema in my feet and legs, there also was increasing damage to my knees that had never fully healed from the crash after my shoot-down.

When we began again, it was just Elbert and I traveling with the two guards, moving along as usual in a crowd of Vietnamese civilians. On the second day, we passed a large contingent of NVA soldiers with heavy weapons and heading south. Usually the troops didn't recognize us, but if one noticed who we were they would sometimes poke us with their walking sticks or try to shove us off the trail into the jungle. I had picked up a few Vietnamese curse words, so when one NVA soldier took a swing at me with his stick and barely missed my head, I glared at him and said, *"Do may,"*—motherfucker. He turned, hate in his eyes, and shook his rifle at me as if he were going to shoot me. One of our guards stepped in between us and settled him down. Then he told me that if I didn't stop that behavior he couldn't protect me. Considering the circumstances, I was thankful for the ironic favor of one NVA protecting me from another. As a precaution for the rest of the walk, the guards made sure that they mingled us in on the side of the group of civilians away from passing units of soldiers.

Time on the trail was generally uneventful if not downright boring. Our guards nonchalantly shouldered their weapons, confident that their two charges weren't going anywhere with all those people around. The civilians, especially the women and children, were almost friendly. Some would chirp out the few English words they knew and smile. They gave us bits of candy and offered cigarettes, which I declined because I didn't smoke, but Elbert eagerly accepted all he could get his hands on. These little acts of kindness and generosity during our long march were the most humane treatment we had received from the Vietnamese through all our years of captivity.

More B-52 Strikes

After two more weeks of walking five or six hours a day and stopping at one of the "pony express stations," we were suddenly ordered to stop. Along the way, we had been forced into nearby bomb shelters, which were all along the trail, to take cover from the devastating B-52 strikes. Right after one of the attacks one afternoon, someone passing us on the trail told us that the camp where we had stayed the night before had been destroyed by bombs. We guessed that our walk had been curtailed by the increased number and severity of the aerial attacks, and they put us into another Laotian hospital. The guards took very good care of us and stayed with us almost constantly as if they feared that someone was trying to get to us. We learned that the Laotians were bitterly angry about the bombing of their villages and wanted to kill us if they had the chance. We were glad that our guards apparently had orders to make sure that we arrived whole and intact wherever they were taking us.

After two or three weeks at the hospital, the bombing had tapered off, and we moved back onto the trail. Almost right away we came upon a cluster of two hundred or three hundred dirty, wounded ARVN soldiers who apparently had been part of an operation into Laos. A South Korean who was with them and who spoke English told us that he and his fellow Koreans were going to be killed because the Vietnamese didn't keep Korean prisoners. I was struck by how cool and matter-of-factly he spoke of his fate. The next day, our guards made a point of taking us near where the ARVNs were being issued packs and weapons. That was the story of that stupid war. The people we went to help to save their country could switch and fight for the other side and not miss a lick. I never saw the South Koreans again and don't know what happened to them, but they didn't deserve to get captured with that bunch.

Later that day, I also saw an American prisoner standing not more than ten feet away by the time I noticed him. He was a warrant officer, a chopper pilot, wearing a fresh flight suit. He was clean, so he hadn't been in captivity very long, and I could see that he was extremely scared. As soon as we saw each other, his guards grabbed him and moved him away very quickly. I never saw him again, but I also never forgot him.

Within a day or two, not fifty yards off the trail in a little clearing, I spotted two abandoned American helicopter gunships. Neither one appeared to be damaged and did not seem to have been there for long. Both had the red-and-white shark-tooth mouth, similar to the Flying Tiger design on old World War II fighters, painted along the side of each chopper's nose. I recognized them as Shark gunships from the 174th Assault Helicopter Company in Chu Lai, but there was no sign of the crews. Obviously, we were in no position to investigate or even ask questions, but I sensed that the warrant officer and two abandoned choppers were indications that Elbert and I weren't the only Americans in the vicinity. There was just no way to know.

Almost four months into our march, we began to leave the relatively flat terrain that runs much of the distance along that stretch of the eastern border of Laos with Vietnam and reached a very mountainous region. Even though we had been traveling at a slow, steady pace, the distance we had been walking once again began to take a toll on our bodies and we started weakening. Elbert's chronic malaria worsened, and my feet and legs were in terrible shape. The already slow journey was slowing even more, and we were doing good to cover five miles a day.

Now we were at the base of the awesome Troung Son mountain range. What stood before us was so tall that its peaks soared into the clouds. The walking was torturous, requiring a full day to climb to the top of each ridgeline, and the ridgelines rose like forbidding barriers. We would walk one day and rest two, usually stopping at the top of a ridgeline to spend the night because the walk down was at least as difficult and painful for us as climbing up, especially as my injured knees became increasingly aggravated and inflamed.

One Step at a Time

After no more than ten minutes of walking, I had to pull one leg up after the other with my hands and arms. Picking our way down to the valleys between ridges, we then would stay for the night before moving up the steep slope of the next ridge. Then we would walk two days before resting for four. At one point, during a stop at one of the stations, a Vietnamese medic injected doses of cortisone directly into my knees to kill the pain. The numbness made the walking almost bearable at the time, but the cartilage damage to my knees from the crash and from walking hundreds of miles became permanent. The pain persists even today.

In all, the trip over the three or four huge ridges that constituted the mountain range took a week. The trail was so steep in places that steps had been cut into the earth and rock and reinforced with bamboo retainers. We rested every half hour on the trail in little cutout areas in the jungle. Had we not been in such physical and mental agony, maybe we would have been able to appreciate and enjoy the beautiful waterfalls that cascaded down the rock precipices for hundreds of feet. Despite the natural beauty of the area, we were absorbed in the painful steps ahead of us and the apprehension of hearing the almost daily thunder of B-52 strikes nearby.

Once we finished our climb over the mountains, we arrived at a camp just inside the jungle at the base. "Tomorrow," the guards said, "we cross the DMZ. You must obey our instructions because we will move very fast." They rested us an extra day. Early the next morning, we set off. That side of the mountains opened into a flat expanse of plains, much of it rice paddies. The guards hustled us along as fast as our bodies would allow, and when we reached a tree line they turned to us and said, "You're in North Vietnam. You're safe now." We could see camouflaged SAM missile positions through the morning mist and knew they were telling the truth.

We walked on a little farther, and suddenly four or five new guards appeared out of nowhere. Everything changed right then. Our guards along the Ho Chi Minh trail and over the mountains had been at least decent if not cordial. These new ones immediately put us in dilapidated handcuffs that were at least forty years old and told us that we were going to walk across the narrow width of the country to Vinh, which is on Vietnam's eastern coast about 150 miles southeast of Hanoi. They took us first to an old concrete, bombed-out house. Handcuffs and chains had been driven into the interior walls of the house, evidence that other prisoners had been held there in the past. Nearby, we saw people from a village, yelling and cursing at us. The guards moved us inside where we spent the night chained to the wall, though we didn't manage to get any sleep. When they unshackled us the next morning, my shoulders and arms were wrenched with the pain of having been elevated all night. The ancient, sharp-edged, rusty cuffs also had cut into our wrists.

When they fed us, the food was altogether different from what we had eaten the last three years. We were given soup and bread. We had not even seen bread in the south or on the march to the north. We were then told that we would leave for Vinh to board a train, but they held us back another day. While at the house, we looked out across the flat terrain where we could hear barrages of antiaircraft fire. We scanned the sky to see if we could see any planes, which we couldn't, but we saw the air bursts exploding at a very high altitude. Whatever they were shooting at escaped the flak.

The next morning we left to begin walking east across the flat, open terrain. After a few days, we arrived at the edge of Vinh where they put us in an old open car, much like an old World War II staff car, and took us to the train station just before dark. Finally, an ancient train pulled in, pulling seven or eight dilapidated passenger cars that reminded me of those used in the old West, open-air and without windows. They put Elbert and me in a cattle car and locked the door, but they didn't chain us. We couldn't see through the wooden siding, except for a faint crack or two. The guards rode in one of the passenger cars.

The ride lasted all night and almost all of the next day, stopping only twice. At one village about forty or fifty Vietnamese stood outside the cars, beating on the side and yelling at us. Through one of the tiny cracks I could see a man holding a primitive pitchfork. Although they couldn't see inside the car, they seemed to know that prisoners were there. They were very agitated and angry, I'm sure, because of the heavy U.S. bombing in and around Vinh, which was one of the Americans' key targets in the north.

The NVA guards, who seemed to enjoy the harassment that they must have known had stricken us with fear, finally dispersed the crowd and opened the door to bring us our meal of soup and bread. When we finished, they locked the door and the train pulled away. Near dinnertime, it pulled into Hanoi. We waited for several minutes before the door opened and the guards ordered us out. They tied a black cloth around our heads as blindfolds, handcuffed our hands in front of us, and led us to an old sedan and put us in the back seat. We drove for less than fifteen minutes and then pulled to a stop. I was able to peek over the blindfold just enough to see in front of us a huge wooden door at the gateway into a walled compound. The big door swung open, and the car drove in. We had finally arrived, I learned within a very short time, at the Plantation, one of the key prisons in the Hanoi system.

10
In Hanoi

Once the car had driven to within ten feet of the great wooden door at the gateway, the driver pulled to a stop at the curb. A guard got out and pounded on the door, which swung open, and the car drove in just past the gate and stopped. The guards opened the car door and told Elbert and me to get out. They removed our blindfolds about the same time someone was closing the gate behind us. The first thing that I noticed was a large, three-story French colonial style villa to the right and behind us. The house faced onto a large courtyard with a big fountain in the middle. The basin of the fountain was about half-filled with green, slimy, stagnant water.

Like most of the other structures laid out at different positions around the compound, the stucco of the villa was a grimy yellow in color and dilapidated from decades of use and poor maintenance. I learned later that it had been the home of Hanoi's Vietnamese mayor during the French occupation. The other pris-

oners referred to it as the "Big House," where the
camp staff had their offices and living quarters.

Just a few yards from the villa was a large bomb
shelter with flowers growing in scattered plots nearby.
Glancing around, I saw that the compound was en-
closed by a brick-and-stucco wall about eight feet tall.
Right in front of me, about thirty yards from the gate,
was a row of low wooden structures that looked like
chicken coops but were actually sheds where individual men were placed. The prisoners called that area
the "Corncrib."

Welcome to the Plantation

On the east side of the courtyard, about fifty feet from
the fountain, was a long, stucco-covered masonry
building with several doors called the "Warehouse."
At the far north end of the open area were several
outbuildings, referred to as the "Gun Shed," that appeared to have been servants' quarters for the mayor
years before. Those buildings were the living quarters
for the American prisoners who had dubbed the entire
complex "Plantation Gardens" or the "Plantation" for
short.

After briefly surveying the area, I looked up and
saw "Doc" Kushner and the other nine prisoners who
had arrived in April. The men looked as if they were
in good health, certainly better than the last time we
saw them, so our hopes of better treatment in Hanoi
already seemed to be paying off.

They were milling around with several others in
the courtyard not far from the fountain, so Elbert and
I joined them in a brief reunion. Because it was nearly
supper time, the visit was cut short while the guards

served soup from a bucket and passed out bread cut into squares. I couldn't say that we had too much to eat, but there was no question that the quality of the food was a definite improvement over the fare we had become accustomed to during the previous three years in the jungle prisons.

After eating, the twelve of us were told to go to our quarters, so Elbert and I followed the others. The large common room provided a three-foot by five-foot pallet for each man to sleep on, and each bed had a small blanket. Because there were so many of us, our room had two defecation buckets instead of just one. We all sat around and began relating our stories of the trip from the south, up the Ho Chi Minh trail, and across North Vietnam. Our visiting apparently went on too long and too loudly to suit the guards, so they yelled at us to be quiet and go to sleep.

The next morning, the guards opened the door and Elbert and I were able to go take a bath. We walked down the length of the building, past fourteen rooms with heavy wooden doors to a big bathing area. A cistern, two feet wide, four feet high, and filled with water, stood on the other side from the entrance to the bathing room. On the floor next to the cistern was a big block of lye soap. We were told to throw water on ourselves and scrub but not to remove our clothes. The Vietnamese were funny that way about modesty.

After several days of walking without having access to a stream and then the two-day train ride, the chance to douse ourselves with water was welcome, but as a "bath" it left a lot to be desired.

That day, after Elbert and I had been issued the standard clothing of two pairs of drab gray-and-red-striped pajamas, a pair of rubber shower-shoe sandals, a mosquito net, and a blanket, the guards began to move people around, putting three or four men to a room in the several cells that made up the Warehouse. Kushner and I were put in a room together, the third one from the end near the bathing area. I guessed that we shared the same room because we were the highest ranking men in our group. After that, we were not to see our other ten prisoners from the jungle until the war was all but over.

Most of the time we were confined to the cells, each of which was outfitted with a squawk box kind of speaker that the camp staff used to transmit radio programming from the Hanoi radio station. Basically, these programs were indoctrination sessions, long narratives about Vietnamese history, and propaganda sessions that they hoped would soften us up. These broadcasts would last as long as five hours a day, but for me at least they were just some noise to help pass the time.

Kushner's Broadcasts

Almost right after Kushner got to the Plantation, the camp staff kept prodding him to read the news over the prison intercom, but he kept refusing. After he and I moved in together, though, he agreed. He told me that he had been going to the radio shack in the Big House and broadcasting news briefs excerpted from Radio Hanoi to the other prisoners. He had made his delivery with a sense of humor to help keep his mind sharp because of the boredom of being confined in the cell so much of the time. Almost right away, we began getting messages delivered in our defecation bucket. "Hold on." "Keep the faith." "We're getting near the end." "Don't do anything for them. Stop what you're doing." That last message, I presumed, was directed at Kushner's broadcasts. At the time, I had no idea where the notes came from or who was writing them. Kushner then told me that the camp had devised secret means of communicating, and it was being conducted by a high-ranking prisoner he had never seen or met. No one from our group in the Warehouse would see him until just before our release in 1973.

The system had been in place for a couple of years before the jungle prisoners arrived and seemed to be crude but well organized. An air force pilot who had been shot down in 1968 and captured in Laos, Lt. Col. Ted Guy, had established a firm military chain of command among the prisoners who were scattered in the Gun Shed and the Corncrib.

As a command officer and a pilot, he was a strict disciplinarian, and he had taken over about two years before I got to the camp. He would circulate written messages to the new jungle prisoners, but he had other means for communicating with the men in the Gun Shed and Corncrib—a tap code, we learned later, that would make the rounds from building to building by a prisoner who would be performing work details assigned by the guards. Those duties included picking up plates and utensils from each cell for washing after meals or emptying and cleaning the defecation buckets. This was a culture that was foreign to the jungle prisoners. For us, after the ordeal in the south that was so often fatally brutal because of disease and malnutrition, there had been virtually no military discipline.

Many of the prisoners who spent their entire captivity in the Hanoi prisons, most of them officers and pilots, later faulted the willingness of some others to do things demanded by the Vietnamese. Such breaches of orders, they thought, undermined the effort to build a strong resistance against the prison staff or the antiwar cause in any way. But after three years of coping with brutal circumstances and making decisions for ourselves, we from the jungle frankly did not easily adapt to that abrupt reintroduction to military ways, especially authority emanating from a commander we had never seen. In addition, most of us weren't doing anything to compromise the code of conduct anyway and were baffled at first by the notes. Besides, our determination to resist became stronger and more resolute after the camp authorities split our group and put us into separate rooms. Still, we very simply declined to accept one of Guy's orders, his insistence that no one accept release if it were offered.

We had become so accustomed to seeing others in our group die that we truly believed that not to go home if the opportunity presented itself was just an acceptance of an eventual death for ourselves. After all we had been through, I don't think anyone in our group of twelve would not have gone home in a heartbeat if offered the chance, which we weren't. But a communication system at least was in place for most of the prison to try to enforce some unity among the POWs. We learned soon enough, though, that Lieutenant Colonel Guy had more problems with prison discipline than we were aware of at the time.

Kushner *did* stop making the broadcasts about three months after I had arrived—for his own reasons, though. He just quit one day, saying, "Why should I do anything for them? They aren't doing anything for me or the rest of us."

I was never asked to make any statements on the radio, but the staff called Kushner and me out many times to write some kind of antiwar or other propaganda message. We would be asked if we would like to write home, and of course we always said yes. Then they would say, "Then first write a statement," and we would refuse. I hadn't written anything useful as propaganda since the political course in Camp Two back in 1968, and the VC found even that unacceptable.

Then one day in early 1972 at the Plantation, the guards brought a *Life* magazine into our cell. One of the articles included a long letter from Kushner's wife, who had just had a baby when he left for Vietnam. She had written a heartfelt, poignant account of the bitter sadness of the years that their child—and others—were growing up without a father. After reading it, I was devastated by her pain and misery, and I told the guards that I was ready to send a letter. I wrote a seven-page open letter to Congress saying, look, we were right to get into the war, and we could and should have won it, but we didn't. Since we didn't, we should get out. I knew there was enough that they couldn't use for propaganda purposes so that they wouldn't mail it, but I got my frustration off my chest anyway.

Just the "Doc" and Me

From August 1971 to May or June 1972, Kushner and I lived with just the two of us in the same room. "Doc" was a really talkative and argumentative fellow, and confrontational conversations were his way of keeping his morale up and staying mentally sharp. When we weren't in our most dire conditions in the south, he and I would strike up similar debates, but our energy level was so low that they didn't last very long. In the Plantation, a good deal of our strength returned. Kushner would argue one position and beat me up one side and down the other, and the next day he would take the opposite position and do the same thing. These sessions began to create tension for me, but they were a way for him to take his mind off everything else.

Then about May, a guard asked me if we wanted new roommates, and I jumped at the chance to bring some variety in to break the tension and monotony. Roger Miller, a warrant officer captured in 1971, and 1st Lt. Dick Anshus, a West Point graduate who had just been taken prisoner, raised our room occupancy to four. I never really spoke much to Kushner after that for the rest of the time we were in Vietnam. Since returning, however, I have seen and talked to him, and we remain friends. I have described our tension at the time of confinement as like being locked in a closet with someone. You'd fight and argue no matter who it was.

Despite all the bitterness and anger directed at the jungle prisoners by some of the pilots who had spent their entire captivity in Hanoi, there was no question that life became far easier there for those of us who had come from the south. After five or six weeks, my health improved greatly. My ankles were better after the edema had subsided and eventually disappeared with the improved diet. I paced around the small enclosure all the time, building up some strength and endurance. By the time of our release in 1973, I was able to do 150 push-ups, although I have to admit that pushing up 110 pounds was easier than the 160 pounds that I weighed when I arrived in Vietnam in 1967.

Dick Anshus was good to have in the room. Not only was he a friendly guy, but somewhere he also had acquired a knowledge of code before he was captured. He had helped get information out of the camp by working some of the code into a few of the letters that the guards would allow to be sent back home.

My first letter home managed to get out, but Anshus's additions to the second and third letters didn't get mailed. The NVA must have figured out that somebody was trying to send code. The letter that I finally succeeded in getting out of Vietnam, though, didn't go through the mail. Ramsey Clark, the former U.S. attorney general and by then a leading war protester, had come to Hanoi in the early summer of 1972 for one of the Vietnamese "See the Famous Sympathetic Americans" shows.

The Plantation had become a showcase prison for visiting American dignitaries. The glum Hoa Lo Prison, better known as the "Hanoi Hilton," was not an appealing setting for a curious world to see the "lenient and humane" conditions in which the POWs were being held, so the Vietnamese converted the old mayor's compound into a more acceptable location to bring in such visitors as Jane Fonda and Joan Baez. No entertainers came to the Plantation while I was there, but the cameras were rolling to catch Clark's visit on film, and when he left he took my letter and several others out of Hanoi by hand.

He took it to New York, where he called my father

at McGuire Air Force Base in Wrightstown, New Jersey, and said, "I have a letter from your son, and I'd like you to come to New York tomorrow and meet with me and the Women's Strike for Peace. I'd like to present you with the letter." My father told me later that he told them to take the letter and "stick it up their ass" for exploiting his son's circumstances for propaganda purposes. About ten days later—and a distance of one hundred miles—the letter arrived in the mail, this time accepted by my strong-willed father.

After Clark left with my letter, I continually asked whether a reply had come from my family. One day a member of the prison staff said to me, "No one wants to write you letters. Everyone in the U.S. is against the war now." The Vietnamese did not bring our letters to us, or at least not to me. My mother wrote and addressed fifteen hundred letters and sent them to Hanoi. None was ever delivered because I never got them. Kushner and I never received any packages from the Red Cross either, although some guys did. We would look out and see someone wearing a sweater or a hat or a pair of socks and wonder where they came from.

Unlike the camps in the south, the Plantation was a holding prison only. The prisoners, except for the rotation of gathering the dirty eating utensils and defecation buckets, were not required to work. Only the men held in the Gun Shed had to make coal balls, molded by hand from coal dust and a kerosene-based paste, that were used for fire fuel in the kitchen. One of the greatest barriers to sanity in such conditions was allowing the mind to go idle, and that was a real challenge for any prisoner.

We no longer had any real fear of dying from malnutrition or disease, and the guards were not physically brutal. But the idleness and sense of isolation from being cramped in one room was a danger to keeping our minds occupied and alert. I passed some of the time reading. The prison staff had a few books that they allowed us to have, and I read *War and Peace* three times. Besides a volume of Shakespeare, I also remember having a copy of *Love Story*. One day, a guard brought Kushner and me a Russian language book. I managed to learn the alphabet and maybe thirty or forty words but not much else because it was a very technical book.

During those seemingly endless days without any creative structure to our lives, we were relieved that at least the constant indoctrination that we experienced in the south did not take place in Hanoi for some reason. That isn't to say that the Vietnamese were not trying to weaken our wills, but that the methods they used were different, as with the interpreter who told me that no one wanted to write to me, or by allowing those of us who did not receive packages to see other prisoners parading around in the goods they had received.

A Harmless Diversion

For a long time I thought that allowing us to listen to the radio was a sort of humane concession by the guards. I could tune in to the daily fifteen minutes of Hanoi Hannah and get a few laughs because I had heard it all before, so it seemed like a harmless diversion. Any news from the "world" that we were allowed to hear was limited to what the Vietnamese wanted us to hear. We were aware of the growing antiwar sentiment in the United States, of course, because it suited the staff's purposes. But the radio also played quite a few songs popular at the time in America, and that was when I became aware that our captors were trying subtly to break down any will to resist. I couldn't have selected sadder songs, given our circumstances, if I had tried to. They appealed to longing for home and to that mournful feeling of love going bad, as with "Make Believe You Love Me One More Time"—all those sentiments that, for a prisoner of war half a world away, eat away at his mind and heart. That was the music that Hanoi Hannah wanted us to hear, and it was painful.

Every man has his limits, and the experience of being a prisoner of war drives each one toward that end. The limit, of course, is that point at which a serviceman finally comes to terms, or not, with abiding by the U.S. Military Code of Conduct by refusing to cooperate with his captors, refusing to accept "special favors," and refusing to assist in giving aid and comfort to the enemy by saying or writing anything that could be used as propaganda against the war effort of his own country.

For some, death is the ultimate limit, as we learned from those who died in the jungles with us. Yet those of us who survived faced the crushing of body, mind, and spirit to the point that we believed our only chance of clinging to the bare thread of life was to yield just enough to survive without betraying our country. If accepting an extra can of condensed milk for the margin of nourishment that would prevent starvation was a special favor, then many of us from the jungle camps were guilty. During our time in the south, only Bobby Garwood was unquestionably collaborating with the enemy, and only Earl Clyde Weatherman was a remote and only temporary possibility, and he most likely was gunned down trying to escape.

Until Kushner read the news for the prison radio in Hanoi, I am aware of no instance in which any statement made by the jungle prisoners I was with was ever used for propaganda purposes. We tried to write them ambiguously so that they would remain as close as possible to compliance with the code of conduct. The writings were clearly coerced, but they did not satisfy the camp commanders and were not sufficiently "progressive" to be published by the VC. Our names did appear on a leaflet that I discovered only recently, but that was not our statement, and it did not bear our signatures, only our printed names. My letter to Congress, even though it was written in a spasm of rage, never left Hanoi because it did not condemn the U.S. war effort and in fact somewhat supported it. Even so, I still regret that I wrote it.

But when we arrived in Hanoi, we discovered an organized group that openly violated the code. These men had formed what was called the Peace Committee or "PC," and they were openly solicitous of the Vietnamese. They flagrantly disobeyed their superior officer's orders to cease their activities, and in some cases they defiantly cursed the senior Americans. They became war resisters, soul mates with their counterparts who demonstrated in the streets at home, and they freely made statements about America's "criminal" conduct of the war.

We had begun to hear from the PCs about the antiwar movement shortly after we got to Hanoi. They had joined it in absentia, or maybe it is more accurate to say that they joined it at the front line. The PCs received favorable treatment from the prison staff for their cooperation, from lemonade and sweets to actually being taken from the prison occasionally for dinner and shows in Hanoi. The prison staff had given them several revolutionary books to study, including the *Communist Manifesto* and works by Mao, Ho Chi Minh, Le Duan, and other such writings by Marx and Engels. The PCs made a point of referring to the hard-core officers such as Guy as "reactionaries" because of their continued efforts to resist any cooperation with the Vietnamese.

Looking for Recruits

They sought to recruit new members from our group during the exercise breaks in the courtyard, and those who refused were ridiculed, most often with the taunt that the holdouts were concerned only with their back pay that could be jeopardized if they were to face a court-martial after they returned home. As a matter of fact, since most of us would be receiving lump sum payments of tens of thousands of dollars, that was one of the incentives many prisoners had for continuing to resist.

Not one of the twelve jungle prisoners was necessarily in favor of the war, but that was only because of the insane way that the United States had been waging it, not because we opposed our government or our country. But only two—Jim Daly and Fred Elbert—joined the Peace Committee. Daly was a Jehovah's Witness and didn't have a hostile bone in his body. He probably considered himself a conscientious objector, but he also was a simple, trusting man, clumsy in more ways than one, who was tricked into joining the army by an unscrupulous recruiter and eventually found himself in the infantry. He had tried, all the way into combat, to plead his case, saying that he refused to kill anyone. When his unit was overrun and he was captured, he had not fired a single shot from his M-16. When he had the chance, with Weatherman, to kill his guard and escape, he refused. In Hanoi, the talk by the PCs of opposing the terrible war lured him into their sway. As for Elbert, whom I never really understood even after several months of walking with him along the the Ho Chi Minh trail, he went into the Big House for several hours one night. When his cellmates returned from the bathing area later, Elbert's belongings were gone. He had moved into a cell with the PCs. After we were finally released, he neither looked at any of the rest of us or talked to us again.

Throughout these activities, Guy still tried to keep a firm grip on the camp, working through his tap code to various parts of the prison to reinforce morale, issue orders, and generally try to keep some semblance of discipline. The Vietnamese managed to break his code more than once, but they could not identify the source of the messages. He would make necessary adjustments, get the word around, and the system went back into operation with a modified code. Then, in early 1972, the PCs informed the NVA guards that the top-ranking officer had been sending orders through the code system. That identified Guy, and he sustained a terrible beating that lasted for five days. By the time the guards were through, he had been reduced to submission. He made a weak statement recorded on tape that was played to the other prisoners on the squawk boxes in their cells that they should obey the NVA guards' orders. His voice was flat and frail, and everyone knew that he had been coerced and didn't mean what he was being forced to say.

The Peace Committee became a sore point of dissension among the prisoners. Its members' apparent antiwar conviction was always balanced in the minds of those of us who weren't associated with them against their desire to save their own skins, which they did at the expense of the rest of us. Guy suffered because of their treachery, but so did others. The Vietnamese had succeeded in breeding conflict among the prisoners by allowing special privileges for the PCs, whose cell doors frequently were unlocked and left open so that they could move around freely whenever they wanted.

One cell that included eight men in our group decided that they would not go into the courtyard if the cell doors of the PCs were open. One day, the guards had ordered that the prisoners in the Warehouse whitewash the dingy walls of their cells. Jose Anzuldua was ordered to fetch a bucket of water to mix the whitewash and saw that the PCs were lounging out in the courtyard, and he returned without the water. The guard was outraged at the disobedience and took Anzuldua to the villa where he was beaten in the kidneys and other areas of his body that would not show cuts and bruises and then placed in solitary confinement for a week. They also took Dave Harker to the interrogation room and slapped him around because the group had disobeyed "the rules" by refusing to associate with the Peace Committee.

Our contempt for the PCs and our resentment for the way they caused trouble for everyone else grew more bitter with each passing week. Even our resident "hippie," Gus Mehrer, who hated rigid military structure, and who I would have thought might share their antiwar attitudes, despised them.

A Spring of Terror

By the spring of 1972, the NVA launched a massive armored attack against the south. President Nixon responded by intensifying U.S. bombing and mining Haiphong Harbor. The renewed heavy bombing in and around Hanoi became our spring of terror, at least as frightening as the artillery and air strikes that forced us to leave the camps in South Vietnam and march north. The Plantation was not far from the main railhead in Hanoi, and for several months we had been watching the NVA moving tanks and supplies in preparation for their spring offensive. They also must have anticipated retaliatory air strikes, because the air-raid sirens blared regularly during practice drills for at least a month before the assault began. When the sirens gave the first genuine warnings around the beginning of April in 1972, everyone assumed that it was just another drill. Then we heard the swoosh-swoosh sound of surface-to-air missiles being launched, followed by the deep "whoomph-whoomph-whoomph" of exploding bombs, at first in the distance and then hitting closer to the prison as the ground shook and the doors and windows of our cells began to vibrate.

For days and nights on end the bombing continued. The prison staff became extremely jittery, and most of us were scared to death. A few of our men took things calmly, but I had been on the receiving end of too many B-52 strikes in the jungle camps and along the Ho Chi Minh trail and was in a state of almost total panic once the sirens sounded and the bombs began falling.

The frequency of the attacks leveled off by mid-summer 1972, and things got more back to normal inside the prison. Occasionally, while we were in the courtyard, we could see the glint of aircraft high in the sky. One day, the guards began cheering wildly and pointing up. There had been a dogfight between an American fighter and an NVA MiG, and an orange parachute was drifting down. All of a sudden, the cheers froze into silence, and the guards began hustling the prisoners back into their cells. I asked Anshus what all the cheering was about and why it stopped suddenly. He just smiled and said, "American pilots don't have orange parachutes."

New prisoners, who had been captured after U.S. planes had been shot down by the SAMs and antiaircraft fire, began coming into the Plantation, bringing the total number to just over eighty. That was about the time that Roger Miller and Dick Anshus joined Kushner and me in our cell. Another was a minor celebrity of sorts, at least to sports fans. Al Krobath of New Jersey had attended The Citadel on a U.S. Air Force scholarship and distinguished himself by becoming the second-leading scorer in college basketball his senior year. Second place didn't count for much except a place in the record books, though, when the top scorer was Lew Alcindor, who later took the name of Kareem Abdul Jabbar. Krobath graduated, but then the air force looked harder at his grades than at his scoring stats and declined his services, so he joined the Marine Corps. Just before he was captured on the outskirts of Hanoi, he had broken his arm after bailing out and was in a large, cumbersome cast. Krobath was among the new arrivals who brought word of what had been happening in the outside world, and the rumors began to spread about the Paris peace talks. Hope began to drift through the prison that maybe the war was nearing an end.

During the sporadic lulls in the bombing throughout the summer of 1972, groups of prisoners were gathered together and taken by the guards to the Hanoi War Museum to see the paraphernalia taken from U.S. planes and the pilots, as well as photographs and propaganda films intended to show how hopeless the American cause had become. I can't honestly say that the trips changed anyone's attitude, but I confess that the self-serving evidence of the war's toll on the men who had been wounded and captured reinforced my bitterness at the tragedy of it all.

Once or twice we also were taken to the Bach Mai hospital, which had been hit in one of the air strikes. The purpose was to show us the "criminal" intentions of the American flyers, but we knew that the damage was accidental. Hell, we had been ordered to avoid hitting targets in the south that had none of the humane value of a hospital, and I knew from my own experience that U.S. pilots avoided taking out easily targeted hospitals like the one I stayed in on the Ho Chi Minh trail. This war, like all others, was ugly.

Then one night in October, an American bomb struck the French Embassy, and the bombing stopped the next day. The cease-fire lasted until well into December, but the NVA persisted in moving men and weaponry into the south, while at the same time bits and pieces of information fed the prison rumor mill that the talks in Paris were breaking down.

More Bombs to Come

Somehow, the prison authorities sensed that the days of quiet in the skies over Hanoi were numbered. The air-raid drills began again. On December 18, 1972, fed up with North Vietnamese intransigence in Paris, President Nixon ordered the beginning of Operation Linebacker Two, the unrelenting "Christmas bombing." A couple of days after the strikes began, a guard came to the window of my cell and said, "Tsk, tsk, Nixon very bad." An hour later, I heard a key in the door and the guard and an interpreter came in and told us, "You must dig," and handed us a big kitchen spoon. We told them that there was no way we could dig through the concrete floor with a damn spoon, so they left and came back in a few minutes with a pickax.

We began taking turns breaking the floor in a ten-foot by four-foot area in the back of the cell. When we had broken through the thin layer of concrete and reached sand and dirt, they took the pick away for someone else to use and told us to use the spoon and whatever else we could find to dig the hole deep enough to act as a shelter against the carpet bombing that pounded the area surrounding Hanoi every half hour through the night, causing the walls and floors to shake from the concussion.

One morning, the day before the attacks started, one of the guards came to our cell and said, "Nixon has solved the POW problem. He's going to kill you and us, too." That night, Linebacker Two began, and the bombs got progressively closer.

After all our digging, the guards told us on December 20 to pack up our belongings. Within a half hour, they blindfolded us, put us into trucks, and took us to the Hanoi Hilton. The Hoa Lo Prison was much larger than the Plantation and closer to the center of Hanoi. Many civilians had gathered with bundles outside its walls, apparently thinking that was a relatively safe place to be. Once inside, we were assigned to a section of buildings we later called "Little Vegas," which was separated from the pilots who stayed in a different area in the Hilton. We were locked immediately in cells. That night, pacing in my cell, I saw through the window my first B-52 blown out of the sky by a SAM. The huge red-orange fireball I thought at first was a nuclear detonation. "Holy shit," I muttered to myself, "he nuked 'em."

On Christmas Eve, 1972, the bombing stopped from six in the evening until ten on Christmas morning, when it resumed and continued for seven or eight days. Near the end, the guards brought us one at a time to the villa where we met the new commander and his interpreter, a truly nasty man we called "Rabbit." The commander showed me a Hanoi newspaper that, if not that day's edition, appeared to be very current. On the front page was a photograph of ten to twelve U.S. crewmen with flight suits and no head gear. Almost all were bandaged, and three were missing arms and one had a stump for a leg with his flight suit tied around it. I was struck by the picture, because I never saw an amputee the whole time I was in captivity. In fact, of the 591 men who returned during Operation Homecoming, none was missing any limbs or had any serious disfigurement. I could only assume that the commander intended for the other prisoners to know that there were other Americans being held separately and that we would share that information with U.S. officials when we returned. Nearly thirty years later, those men—and others—have not been accounted for.

Finally, near the end of the month, things got very quiet. The prisoners were still kept locked in their cells, but the attitude of the guards relaxed noticeably. We began asking if the war was about to end, and they would answer, "Maybe, maybe." On December 30, the doors all opened in our area, and the camp commander called sixty or seventy of us out into formation. He was smiling. "I have some news that I'm not supposed to tell you until tomorrow, but I'm going to. The war is over. The United States has surrendered."

He waited for our reaction. Without any prearranged plan, we all turned around in unison and walked in silence back to our rooms. Then somebody started laughing. The prison staff began surveying us to discover what had triggered the laughter and noticed that some of us were looking at the flagpole. Some inattentive prison guard had raised the North Vietnamese flag upside down, which is a recognized distress signal. Immediately, a guard ran to the pole, shinnied up it, and corrected the mistake. We suppressed our laughter as best we could at the comic scene, and the commander stood there trying to fathom the meaning of our reaction. I'm not sure that any of us could have told him for sure. That was the craziness of it all. We had hoped for release so many times in the past, had those hopes dashed by the cynicism of our captors, and now weren't sure what to believe. On more than one occasion, Rabbit had said, "Some of you won't return."

A Dilemma for Some

But the members of the Peace Committee faced a serious reckoning. Some of them really wanted to stay behind and enlist in the NVA, and they went to the prison commander and sought to decline their release. Apparently the Vietnamese didn't want any last-minute surprises that could have created a public relations crisis and jeopardized the prisoner release, which was just one step in their long-range plan for American withdrawal. The PCs were told they had to leave with the rest of us. Just being in the same prison with men like that who were willing to reject their country contributed to the grim sense of uncertainty and apprehension among our group.

The next day, all the men in the entire prison were brought into the open area for a big celebration with Vietnamese musicians, dancers, singers, jugglers, and clowns. That was the first time I had seen where the pilots lived. The Vietnamese brought out a banquet, and from that day until we departed the food was well prepared, with meat every day, and was served in generous portions. Obviously, they were fattening us up for the cameras.

Rabbit, the interpreter, came up to me one day and said, "We have been enemies for many years, and now we are friends. What do you think?" I looked at him coldly and replied, "I don't think anything. I want to go home."

Within a few days, members of the International

Control Commission from Sweden, Germany, and Canada came into the prison to inspect and evaluate our conditions. The Vietnamese had placed fruit baskets and little bowls of candy in each cell to demonstrate how well we had been treated by the humane staff. The Red Cross packages were rushed in, filled with candy, gum, and books. Still, though, many of us received no mail. The guards told us that no one wanted to write to us.

After the international inspectors finished touring the prison, we were broken into groups for the return. Robert Lewis and Jim Pfister, the crew members who had been shot down with me five long years before, were assigned to the second group. I assumed that I would be going with them since we had been together for the duration of our captivity, but I was placed in the third group. Rabbit walked up to me and smiled as he said, "We like you very much. Maybe the war will start up again and we can keep you several more years." They never let up.

During the period from the announced cease-fire until I left on March 13, 1973, the Vietnamese used the time to pack in as much influence on us as they could. They loaded us in jeeps or small buses to tour Hanoi to see the devastation of the American bombing. The train station was totally destroyed. We went by the Bach Mai hospital again and saw the wreckage of a B-52 a few blocks away from the Hilton. As we drove back through the streets of downtown, the civilians would cheer as we passed, not so much in triumph but with friendliness. One young woman handed a man in my jeep a flower as if to say that the war was over, so let's be friends.

The Big Day, Finally

As the appointed day for my departure neared, the prison staff began to return personal property to us. I had received a receipt after my shoot-down for my watch and an air force ring that had belonged to my father. I sold the watch in Camp One to a guard for an extra portion of some food, but the guards at the Hilton couldn't account for my ring. Belligerent to the end, I yelled, "You'd better find my ring because I'm not going home without it!" The other guys thought I'd gone crazy. The guards searched again, without success, so I relented and went home without it.

Lieutenant Colonel Guy, ever the strict commander, issued orders that everyone would wear the gray windbreaker jackets we had been issued with the front zipped exactly halfway. Each man would carry the small ditty bag in his left hand, leaving his right hand free to salute. On March 13, twenty-two of us loaded onto a bus for the trip to the airport. With the terminal in view, the bus stopped, and an interpreter walked to the building to confer with some officials. Looking out the window, I was surprised that the Hanoi airport was left untouched during the weeks of bombing, as if there would be a need to use it soon. The Vietnamese official came back within three or four minutes to say that there was a problem and that we may have to go back to the prison, but within another ten minutes the bus started again, and we drove to the side of the terminal and unloaded. In fifteen minutes, we heard the engines of the C-141s coming. The three big planes, with a fighter escort overhead, came in for a low-level flyby, circled, and landed.

The prisoners stood on the tarmac in line by a table where Rabbit sat smiling. A few yards away and facing us was the American side where a microphone sat on a table. As each man's name was called, he stepped forward, and an officer who was walking from the other side met him midway between the two tables to escort him onto the plane. Two female nurses were on each plane to meet us, and the smell of their perfume—after so many years—filled me with a confusing numbness that was part joy, part relief, and part ecstasy.

We fastened our seat belts as the pilot taxied to the end of the runway. As he threw the engines into full throttle, and the plane lifted off the ground, the newly freed prisoners erupted in a roaring cheer, surpassed only by the one that greeted the pilot's announcement, "Gentlemen, we have just left Vietnamese airspace."

11
Home Again

As elated as I was to be released, I did not realize what lay ahead in the transition from five years as a prisoner of war in primitive Vietnam to an American citizen returned to the most advanced, prosperous country in history. When the airplane climbed away from Hanoi, headed for Manila, I hadn't yet given much thought to the details of such an adjustment. Freedom itself was reward enough that first day. Like many others who had been held prisoner, I was unsure of what I was going home to.

We had been kept informed during captivity of the growing U.S. antiwar feeling. The war had already forced Lyndon Johnson to withdraw from seeking another term as president soon after I had been captured, and when George McGovern appeared to have so much political support early in the campaign of 1972 I began to wonder how the American people would feel toward us, the prisoners, when we came home. Most of the time I expected that we would probably be slipped quietly into the country and sent as quickly into obscurity as possible to shove the war and its reminders into the history books.

Our arrival at Clark Air Force Base in Manila erased any lingering fears of rejection. A large crowd of American military personnel and civilians met the plane when we arrived and gave us a rousing, warm welcome. The same reception would greet us later when we arrived in the United States.

Five Years Without a Bath

For three days, we were assigned to the base hospital where we received extensive medical examinations. After we were assigned to hospital rooms, the first order of business was to hand each man a scrub brush and a bar of soap. "There is the shower," I was told, "and you can't come out until the bar is gone." Five years without a good bath had left us pretty ripe, although we had grown so accustomed to ourselves that we didn't notice.

After taking our showers, we were directed to the mess hall, which was open twenty-four hours a day. As I walked in behind a colonel, the first thing I saw was a huge bowl of rice. The colonel grabbed the bowl and threw it across the room and said loudly, "There'll be no goddamn rice for my men!" As I looked at the incredible selection of food, I had a sudden craving for a peanut butter and jelly sandwich, but by the time I had finished ordering, I had before me four eggs, a T-bone steak, a milk shake, a banana split—*and* a peanut butter and jelly sandwich. Miraculously, I didn't have a bit of trouble with my intestinal tract as a result.

For the next two days, we spent most of our time undergoing further medical tests, opening and reading mail that had been delivered to us, and shopping in the base exchange, which gave us a 10 percent discount on our purchases. Besides receiving a haircut and manicure, each man also was allowed a thirty-minute telephone call back home. A couple of the more daring among us slipped out one night to explore the raunchy marvels of Manila, so guards were posted thereafter at our doors to make sure that we were afforded the proper "security."

After three days, we were assigned to a stateside installation where we would be debriefed and receive more detailed medical examinations. By the time I arrived four days later at McGuire Air Force Base in New Jersey, I hadn't slept since the night before we left Hanoi because I was so hyped up. When I stepped down from the plane at McGuire, three helicopters were waiting and a crowd was gathered behind some retaining ropes. I was met by a colonel, who shook my hand and told me that I could make a few remarks at the microphone placed on the tarmac but that he was under orders to get me to the hospital at nearby Fort Monmouth as soon as possible.

After thanking everyone for coming to meet me and saying how glad I was to be home at last, I turned to leave. All of a sudden, some people broke under the ropes and came running toward me—three cousins and an uncle who hugged me and told me to hurry because my parents and other members of the family were waiting at the hospital. I climbed into one of the helicopters with the captain who had been assigned to me as my escort in the Philippines. He would be joined by another captain at Fort Monmouth. The two of them were never out of my sight for the entire time until my tests and debriefing were finished. The captain told me during the chopper ride that the preliminary tests showed that I was generally fine and that I had all my back pay waiting for me. Life was looking awfully good by then.

Within thirty minutes, we landed at the headquarters pad at Fort Monmouth. I was greeted by a two-star general and put into his staff car for the two-minute drive to the hospital, which had been decorated with signs and welcome-home banners that kids from the local school had made. My parents, brothers, sisters, and extended family were in my room when I walked in, and we had a wonderful reunion. They all looked so different, but then I guess I did, too, after five years.

A couple of hours later, the doctor came in and said that I needed to get some rest, so my family went to the visiting officers quarters where they would stay for the next several days while I was in the hospital. By then, I had gone sleepless for four days. After three more days of medical tests, I was still too wound up emotionally to fall asleep, so the doctor finally came in and told me that he was going to put me to sleep with a big pill and a needle. That was at two in the afternoon. When I woke up, the clock read seven—but it was the next evening, twenty-nine hours later. The rest was essential, the doctor said, to clear my head so that I could begin my debriefing.

Two army intelligence officers spent six days exhaustively examining everything I could remember about my years in captivity. As the days passed, I became somewhat grouchy from the ordeal, not because of the debriefers but because everyone else was through with theirs in about half a day. I learned later that mine was by far the most extensive of any prisoner held in the jungle camps of the south, probably because I could read aerial maps and had a general idea of where I was held all those years.

A Murky Realm

As the sessions ran one into the other, I realized that the questioners knew far more about me and the circumstances of my captivity than even I did. By the time the debriefing was over, I had been introduced to a murky realm that I could not understand, a realm where my destiny could have been entirely different if certain official decisions had been made or not made.

The first two hours of the first day, my debriefers devoted their questions to my general recollections, and I told the officers that I could remember the first day and the last day but that all the others ran together. Then they began to probe more specifically about events. They asked first about the men who came back, and when I got ahead and mentioned some of those who did not return, they kept saying that we would move on to that subject later. They were extremely methodical and knew exactly how to drag their fine-tooth comb through my memory.

On the third day, they brought in very detailed maps of the Que Son Valley, where I had been shot down and captured, and laid them on the floor. Although it was impossible in the jungle to orient myself to any exact location, I had a general idea of where the camps were in relation to the place where I had been shot down. I also knew that we were always near a river and that we had been moved basically to the west. The officers pointed to the location on the map where I had been captured and asked me to show them where we had walked. I began to detect that their questions were leading me to confirm what they already knew, that they had some kind of documented information indicating where I had been.

A few years later, I learned from Mark Leopold, a gunship pilot in my company, that within a day or two of my shoot-down he and others had tracked us for a couple of weeks. They used a "sniffer" machine mounted in a helicopter that would fly over the jungle. The Geiger counter-like machine contained powerful sensors that could detect body chemicals from urine, and high concentrations indicated by electronic impulses would signal the presence of several people. Leopold told me that infantry teams, alerted to our possible positions by data gathered from the "sniffing" choppers, had set three ambushes to try to rescue us where they thought we would be. Things just didn't work out according to plan. Unfortunately, I also learned that monkey urine also set off the meter on the machine.

I told the debriefers that my father, who was an air force colonel with access to the Pentagon, had been advised of my probable capture within a week, but that Lewis's family did not receive confirmation until late in 1969, after the release of Watkins, Strickland, and Tinsley. I asked how the Pentagon knew about my capture, but all that the debriefer said was that "we have people out there, not necessarily Americans." I couldn't escape the conclusion, which I kept to myself, that the Pentagon knew a great deal more about missing soldiers than it was willing to tell, even to the family of a captured army helicopter crew chief.

By the third day, I was becoming more irritable and began complaining about the tedious sessions and their requests for minute details of seemingly insignificant issues that were hard to remember. The sessions went on for four or five hours in the morning after my medical tests and continued for another four or five hours in the afternoon after lunch. Every time I tried to bring up Bobby Garwood and Earl Clyde Weatherman, the debriefers kept saying that they were going to be covered in another category and that we would get back to them.

But on the fourth day, they turned to the subject of men who did not return. I wanted to bring up Garwood, but they said not yet, talk about Weatherman first. He seemed more like a confused young kid rather than a crossover, I said, and he had a mysterious aura about him. After mentioning as many personal conversations with him as I could remember, I said that he was dead, killed in the escape attempt in 1968. The debriefer then looked at me and said, "Are you sure?" He asked in a way that left me with the impression that he was not completely sure, but when I said that was what we were all told by Denny Hammond, who was with him at the time, they didn't discuss Weatherman anymore.

A Subject of Interest

"Who else besides Garwood?" they asked. We had heard of McKinley Nolan, supposedly a black crossover who had joined the VC and fought with them against Americans, but I'd never seen him. When I

mentioned seeing the recently captured warrant officer on the Ho Chi Minh trail in Laos, the debriefers'
interest suddenly perked up. They asked if I could
identify him. I said I thought so. The next day, they
brought in two large books, photo albums like police
mug shot files. I looked through hundreds of faces.
After I had gone through all the pages without rec-
ognizing the pilot, they began to go back and point
to specific photos.

When that search failed to produce results, they put
the books aside and produced a five-inch by seven-
inch photograph. It was a black-and-white, high-
resolution picture of a man walking toward the
camera lens, which was below the level of the ground
where the man was walking. I studied it carefully for
two or three minutes and then said that I could not
recognize him and had no idea who he was. The two
debriefers looked at each other and smiled, and one
of them said, "It's you." I said that of course it wasn't
me, and they said *oh yes it is.* Then I stared long and
hard again. Finally, as if a veil were lifting, I ac-
knowledged in surprise, "It is me!"

The picture had been taken during the march up
the Ho Chi Minh trail. I hadn't seen myself in a mir-
ror for three years by then, and I had no idea I looked
that bad—emaciated, hunched over, face drawn. I
asked the obvious, "Who took it?" They smiled again
and said, "We really can't tell you that." Once again,
I'd learned that my country knew exactly where I
was.

After putting the photo back into a folder, the debriefers asked if I was aware of anyone in the north
I had heard about who had not returned. I recalled
that a civilian consultant who had been captured in

Hue during the 1968 Tet offensive was being held at the Hanoi Hilton while I was there. He told me that his group had talked through the wall of his cell to a group of B-52 pilots in the adjoining cell who had been captured during the Christmas bombing of 1972. They were tending to some crewmen who were seriously wounded, he said, some of them with missing limbs. He said they told him the most seriously wounded would be taken from the prison and released separately.

The debriefers asked me if I believed him, and I said "Why not?" I had seen the newspaper in the prison commander's office with the front-page photograph of the amputees, so the connection seemed logical. Then they asked, as if this were surprising news, "You saw this newspaper?" I answered yes and then asked them pointedly, "What's being done to get these men back?" After a long pause, one of the debriefers said, "We know there are people still there. We're doing all we can. It's just going to take time."

As the years have passed since that day, I have discovered that far more was known in high places than I realized and that the explanation, "It's just going to take time" appears to be an open-ended proposition.

Let's Talk About Garwood

On the fifth day of the debriefing, the officers brought in some other photo albums, a pad of drawing paper, and the maps once again. "Now," they said, "let's talk about Garwood." I explained as fully as I could remember the ten to twelve occasions that I spent time with him or had conversations with him. Then they began to bore in, asking for more details. Did he have any pictures, medals, nail clippers, stamps? I said that I remembered that he carried an old wallet but that I never got close enough to him because, basically, I tried hard to stay away from him.

Others had seen his possessions, but I avoided him for the entire time that I knew him. He had been responsible, I was sure, for urging the camp commander in the jungle to make Kushner, Harker, and me—when we were at our sickest and weakest—dig a bomb shelter because we were "lazy Americans." Had I any recollections of specific instances when Garwood used the bullhorn, and how many times had I seen him carrying a rifle, the debriefers asked. I personally never saw him with the bullhorn—McMillan had said that he did—but my memory of specific times and places that he carried a rifle was just too blurry. I simply knew that it was several, probably about ten.

He most certainly, though, was not one of us, and I made several references to his being an opportunist. He learned Vietnamese and spoke it fluently, made himself useful as an interpreter, acted as a messenger, guarded the other prisoners, and helped teach the political course. In his own selfish interest, he stole chickens from the VC guards and shared his tobacco. I believed all of his efforts to ingratiate himself with some American prisoners were to gather information about the rest of us.

The debriefing officers and I talked all day about Garwood. I was nearly exhausted, and my voice was giving out. Earlier, I had asked why they wanted so many detailed answers, whether they might know where he was, or whether they already had him. The debriefers had ignored my questions, but at the end of the day they asked, "If we can ever get our hands on him, would you testify against him?" I recalled for them my promise to the dying Denny Hammond that I would tell the world the truth about what happened. With that, the debriefing for that day was over.

The next day found my voice still almost gone. The officers brought in a chalkboard so that I could write short answers for them. After lunch, they brought in a big envelope and set it down on the table with the hand-drawn maps I had made for them earlier of the four jungle camps where we were held. One by one, they pulled large glossy photographs from the envelope and laid them next to each one of my pencil-drawn maps.

They had aerial photographs of every camp and remarked how accurately I had recalled the details of each one, including a tree in Camp One with initials carved in it. We discussed the photo of Camp Four, and I told them that one night I had stepped out of the hootch to try to see the full moon through the jungle canopy. All of a sudden, a shadow passed over me through the silvery light like a faint gray stream of smoke, and the low drone of a motor no louder than a lawn mower drifted by overhead. Next morning, I told the other guys that I thought a spy plane had been taking our pictures. That was shortly before the failed rescue attempt, but I couldn't be sure if there was a correlation. The debriefers didn't show me any photos taken at night with an infrared camera.

Even so, these companion renderings of the camps—my crude pencil drawings, their high-definition photos—were shocking to me because the military date and time that the photographs were taken by the reconnaissance planes were printed in the margin, and each corresponded to the time I was in each camp. In hoarse amazement I asked, "If you knew where I was, why didn't you come and get me out?" One of them looked me right in the eye and responded, "We don't know. That's not our job. I can't give you an answer."

At the time, the knowledge of the photographs left me mystified, curious, and angry. Still, I was being treated royally in the hospital, and things were going so well that all I had learned in the previous six days hadn't fully sunk in yet. Besides, I was exhausted and voiceless from the intensive interviews and was glad that it was finally over.

What Radio Broadcasts?

During the course of my debriefing, one of the officers asked me, "Did you make any broadcasts?"

"No," I answered emphatically.

"Are you sure?" he asked again.

I repeated that I had not, but I was curious about the way he asked the question. The interviewers dropped the issue at that point and never brought it up again, and frankly I hardly gave the matter another thought for nearly twenty-five years.

Then just before this book was to go to press in April of 1997, I was surfing randomly through Internet web sites when I happened onto the Library of Congress POW/MIA database. After entering a few key words, I decided to enter my own name to see whether there were any entries on my captivity. The response that flashed onto my computer screen stunned me. There were thirteen distinct references, four of which were especially disturbing to me because the headlines on the data entry sheet read "broadcasts" or "radio broadcasts."

Within a week, I was able to obtain through the photocopy division of the Library of Congress copies of the documents referred to on the Internet relating to supposed events involving my broadcasting propaganda statements. I have the texts, contained in official U.S. intelligence reports, of two messages that I supposedly read over the air—statements that not only did I never make but that I also had never heard of until recently. One appears to be an expanded version of an actual letter home that I was allowed to write and send to my parents. I never read that letter, nor this longer version of it, over the radio. The other document is a three-page "Christmas greeting" that I allegedly read over Hanoi Radio in late December of 1971. I never read that letter, either, nor had I ever seen it until recently. The language, stilted and brittle, obviously was not mine, but because the intelligence reports indicate that the broadcasts were made by a male with an American accent I can only speculate that one of the members of the Peace Committee in the same prison was enlisted by the Vietnamese to pose as me to make the broadcasts.

I have never denied writing or signing some of the statements that I did while I was a POW. Under duress, abuse, and torture, almost all of us who returned have admitted our failings, and most of us regret them. But I never made a radio broadcast, and now I have learned that my government has official intelligence files available for public viewing falsely indicating that I did. I shudder to think of the unjust damage that could befall any citizen's good name and reputation because of such erroneous reports. I believe that I, and countless others wrongly accused in those files, have a right to expect such documents now in the public domain to reflect the truth.

Getting Back to Work

In all, I spent three weeks at the hospital. Then I was given leave to go home to New Jersey and become reacquainted with the American way of life, which I did for almost a full year. I spent a lot of time with my family and bought a car. I visited old friends and traveled to see some army buddies back in Texas. Like other former POWs, I received many gifts, including two trips to Orlando, which I took with different members of my family, and a cruise and a golf trip to Myrtle Beach, which I didn't take.

Major League Baseball gave me a lifetime pass, which has allowed me to see more than two thousand games all around the country. The Philadelphia Phillies, my original hometown team, were especially kind to me, and I didn't miss a home game the first two years after I returned. I also gave talks to schools and civic clubs about my experiences.

All the former POWs were required to receive monthly psychological evaluations. After four or five months, I went to the office of the army major who was to examine me at Fort Monmouth. He hadn't arrived yet, so I sat in his swivel chair to test it out and was spinning around when he walked in, flabbergasted at what he saw. I returned his chair, and he just asked me how I felt. "Sir," I answered, "I'm more sane than you are." He shook his head, signed off my clearance, and dismissed me. He probably figured that I was just strange anyway.

After a few months, I began calling my case officer in the POW office at the Pentagon and asking when I could go back to work. We would talk for a few minutes, then he would tell me to take another month off and call back. Finally, in March 1974, almost a full year since I had returned, I was assigned to the Lakehurst Naval Air Station, flying helicopters that were performing research and development tests of electronic equipment.

In the meantime, Sharon Sanders, the sister of Charlie Sanders, who was one of my former door gunners with the Firebirds, introduced me to Jane LaCon. On August 3, 1974, Jane and I were married in Corpus Christi Catholic Church in Burlington County, New Jersey, where she grew up. She was, and remains, the best thing that ever happened to me. Life was back to normal: I had begun a family, I had returned to flying, and I was living in my old stomping grounds.

Then in late 1976, a colonel in the warrant officer branch at the Pentagon called and said that it was time for a long-tour overseas assignment, which is required for career servicemen. I told him that I had done more than my share of overseas assignments—six of the last nine years, in fact, at one "duty station." He informed me that, according to my army records, I got credit for only six short tours in Vietnam, and I needed a long tour. I hung up. He called back and said something about being cut off, then began almost pleading with me. He offered me the cushiest assignments, Hawaii, Germany, anywhere in the world I wanted. I told him to send me to Fort Dix, which is in New Jersey, twenty miles away from Lakehurst. The next day he called and said OK, and in early 1977, I joined a VIP flight detachment ferrying generals and colonels between New Jersey, the Pentagon, and helipads along the Hudson River in New York. There was a lot of spit and polish that went with the job, but it was a lifetime away from the five-year nightmare of Vietnam. Those memories had begun to lose their painful edge. Then one evening on the TV news, it all came rushing back when the screen glowed with the image of a familiar face: Bobby Garwood.

12
Garwood Court-martial

Nothing out of the ordinary interrupted the routine of the assignment that proved to be so satisfying for me at Fort Dix. Flying had become my professional reason for being, and it was second only to my family in the order of my life's priorities. The army had found a way to squeeze some generosity out of its rigid regulations on foreign duty assignments and allowed me to do what I loved doing in a region of the country that, for all practical purposes, was in the neighborhood I had called home since I was a boy.

Two new presidents had taken office since I had returned from the war, and most of the festering national anger and disillusionment from the war had been eased into the recesses of most people's memories by new concerns in 1979. The U.S. economy was being whiplashed by inflation, and Cold War tensions with the former Soviet Union were never far from the surface. If anyone paid attention to Vietnam at all, it was because of its invasion of Cambodia at the first of the year.

In late March 1979, after returning home one evening from the base, I had flipped on the six o'clock news. I was astounded to see film footage of a familiar face that accompanied the story on the return of a man who had been taken prisoner during the Vietnam War and suddenly emerged after fourteen years. Bobby Garwood looked much as I had remembered him in the jungle, but as the news program revealed, he could barely speak English. He didn't say much in the few seconds that he appeared, but his words were clipped with a heavy accent. Jane, my wife, and I discussed him for a few minutes, and she asked whether the Marine Corps would court-martial him. I said that I couldn't imagine anything else.

A Sympathetic Press

From the beginning of Garwood's return, I had been surprised at the attitude of the press in covering the story. Every article I read suggested that here was this poor guy who spent fourteen years as a prisoner in Vietnam, and with the Marine Corps planning to prosecute him for treason, desertion, and a host of other offenses, that surely what he had been through was enough. He was, the stories said, just another prisoner in a survival situation. What! I couldn't believe it. Didn't they know he guarded the other prisoners, interpreted for the Vietnamese, threatened the prisoners, and spied on them? My initial reaction to the Garwood story was frustration and concern that the truth was not forthcoming, but within a week the fanfare died down. Six years had passed since other POWs and I had documented Garwood's actions for the record, and the press and public seemed to have no clue about the reality of what the man had done.

In April 1979, I received a call from the Marine Corps Judge Advocate General's office asking me to give a written statement about my knowledge of Garwood's activities while I was a prisoner of North Vietnam and the Viet Cong. I immediately agreed and met at Fort Dix on April 12 with two agents of the Naval Investigative Service. The ensuing six-page statement basically recounted my firsthand experiences with Garwood during the eighteen months or so that he and I were in the same camps.

I went to great pains not to exaggerate particular incidents and concentrated only on events and situations that I had personally witnessed. I distinguished, for instance, between Garwood's carrying an AK-47 rifle and his aiming it directly at any American prisoners because I never saw him actually do so. I pointed out that he had not, to my knowledge, interrogated any prisoners, even though I was sure that his one-on-one "conversations" with us were subtle efforts to extract information useful to him, if not to the camp cadre, and probably both.

I tried to be fair by including the contradictory comments Garwood had made about whether he wanted to return to the United States or stay with the Vietnamese and help them in their "struggle." At one time, he had said that he wanted to stay and help because he was upset by the killing of all the children, although he didn't say what he meant by "help." He talked about America and good food, but I never heard him say that he wanted to return. At another time, he told me that he had been in voice range of

American troops and vehicles while he was out in the bush but was afraid to escape to reach them because he had another guard with him.

The unwritten message in my statement was that Garwood had to be judged by what he did, not by what he said. Even at that, in all honesty, I harbored some sense of concern, if not really sorrow, for Garwood and his precarious situation. As deeply as I believed that he had a very serious accounting to make for the decisions he had made in Vietnam, no one should take any relish in seeing another person have imposed on him the enormous psychological and emotional ordeal of a court-martial.

Similar statements were being taken from other former prisoners around the country in anticipation of a court-martial. Why Bobby Garwood should be prosecuted when so many others had also collaborated with the enemy was a question that many people asked. In Hanoi, Adm. James Stockdale, one of the highest-ranking officers in captivity, and Lt. Col. Ted Guy clearly intended to bring charges against those, especially members of the Peace Committee, whose actions they believed violated the code of conduct. In fact, Guy tried unsuccessfully to have several men brought up on charges.

Loss-Cutting Time

That decision, however, had already been made at the highest levels in the Pentagon. For the policymakers, Operation Homecoming in early 1973 was loss-cutting time, an opportunity to get all American soldiers home so that the war, or at least the direct U.S. involvement in it, could be put behind the country.

Before the first plane carrying the newly released prisoners lifted off the runway in Hanoi, the decision was already final that no punishment would be meted out for the men who issued propaganda statements or otherwise collaborated with the Vietnamese.

Part of the ruling was both logical and reasonable, and I personally benefited from it, as did hundreds of others. The physical, mental, and psychological brutality with which the Vietnamese treated the prisoners forced virtually everyone beyond the limits of endurance. The code of conduct had been written with the assumption that prisoners of war would be under the control of a rational enemy willing to abide by international law. The Vietnamese were neither rational nor humane.

Even Ted Guy, beaten horribly while we were at the Plantation, submitted to the pressure that, under the strict dictates of the code of conduct, left him in technical violation. Garwood's defenders argued that his circumstances were different only in degree. In the final analysis, though, no one was court-martialed right after Operation Homecoming because the Pentagon and the White House didn't want to interfere with burying as quickly as possible every reminder of the only war that the United States lost, a war that had badly divided the nation in the process.

In the final analysis, however, the U.S. military did not lose the war on the battlefield in Vietnam, not even during the 1968 Tet Offensive when the Viet Cong infrastructure was virtually destroyed. The United States began losing the war in the press and on nightly television news, then effectively lost it at the Paris peace talks. The political healing could not proceed as long as the wound remained open, and protracted legal proceedings against former prisoners would only keep memories of the war fresh and the wound open. In 1973, the government just wanted the country to forget about Vietnam. That meant writing certain things off.

A Marked Man

For the marines, though, Garwood had chosen to reject his allegiance to their motto, "Semper Fideles"—always faithful. They went after him with a vengeance. From the time in late 1978 in Hanoi when he successfully slipped a note to a Finnish diplomat saying that he wanted to go home, Garwood was a marked man. Declassified government documents, however, indicated years later that U.S. defense intelligence had tracked his whereabouts throughout the war and since, virtually until the day he flew out of Vietnam and met a military escort in Bangkok. As he boarded the aircraft that was to take him home, he was immediately ordered to "shut up" and say nothing, and then he was read his rights. From that point until the following November, the marines began a laborious investigation of Garwood to determine the extent of the charges that could be brought against him.

They began to dig into all the debriefing reports that we prisoners had given in 1973, referring in any way to Garwood. That search resulted in my being contacted and asked to make my April 1979 statement, which was the foundation of the testimony I was to give later in the year at a preliminary hearing and in the court-martial—one of the longest and most expensive in history that lasted from September 1980 until February 1981. But the marines' investigation of 1979 seemed to drag on interminably, from April until late November, and in the end it produced a file that was reported to have been two and a half feet thick.

During it all, Garwood was assigned to Camp Lejeune, North Carolina, where he sorted mail and performed clerical tasks. The marines treated him as a pariah, and he became reclusive, spending most of his time in the barren simplicity of his barracks room. The government had withheld the $145,000 in back pay that had accumulated in his fourteen-year absence. Behind the scenes, the marines built their case against him, and in November they recommended a series of charges: desertion during time of war; soliciting American troops to throw down their arms and refuse to fight; unlawful conversations with the enemy; maltreatment of two other prisoners of war; and acting as an enemy interrogator, interpreter, and guard against his fellow prisoners.

Some charges initially considered were omitted, such as having caused the tortures of Russ Grissett and Ike Eisenbraun. As both of them died in captivity, there were no witnesses. A preliminary hearing, roughly the equivalent of a grand jury proceeding and called an Article Thirty-Two hearing, began the third week in December 1979 to decide whether Garwood should be brought before a court-martial on the charges. Two marine officers had been appointed to represent Garwood, and his father had hired a civilian lawyer, Dermot Foley, who effectively became the lead attorney. Midway through the hearings, the government assigned two new lawyers to the case, Capt. Werner Hellmer and Lt. Theresa Wright. They replaced the original prosecutor, Maj. R. J. Marien, who retired abruptly from the military.

Assisting the Prosecution

During the Article Thirty-Two hearing, I had been released by the army to be available for as long as necessary as a witness at Camp Lejeune. I reported in early December 1979 and started going on my own into the office about eight o'clock each morning to assist the prosecutors in developing the case. I came in wearing a leather jacket and jeans, and the TV crews who were hanging around had no idea who I was. Later, when I took the stand in full uniform, they were all shocked that this source had been right in their midst for days, and they had never asked me a question.

I had been going through my preparation work one day before the testimony was scheduled to begin and decided to take a break and get a drink of water down the hall. During the time I had been in North Carolina I hadn't seen Garwood, but as I stepped down the corridor toward the water fountain, we passed each other and he said matter-of-factly, "Hello, Frank." I responded, "Hello, Bob." That was it, four words after more than ten years. Then, looking at him as he walked on, I thought to myself, "Why don't you just come clean, Bobby? Why don't you just 'fess up?"

The hearing, which was interrupted by Christmas and continued until February 1, 1980, also included testimony from Dave Harker, Ike McMillan, Willie Watkins, Robert Lewis, Gus Mehrer, and Luis Ortiz-Rivera. Each of us had witnessed or experienced different events during the time that Garwood was among us in the jungle, but all of us also reinforced the consistent awareness of the role that he played in relation to the prisoners.

When the questioning and cross-examination were completed, the presiding investigating officer, Maj. Thomas B. Hamilton, rejected the argument by Garwood's military lawyer that the charges be brought before a special court-martial, the equivalent of a misdemeanor court.

In ruling that he would face a general court-martial, Hamilton said, "If believed, the evidence clearly supports the inference that the accused engaged in the conduct alleged for the express purpose of escaping the fate of all the others, who for one reason or another, found themselves in the hands of the enemy. Clearly, their fate ranged from eventual release to death. It is my opinion that the accused should now, if convicted, be placed at the risk of the same spectrum of fate endured by those from whom he freely disassociated himself over a decade ago."

Soon after that ruling, however, the base commandant, most likely under the direction of President Jimmy Carter and the Defense Department, ordered that the death penalty would not be under consideration. Hamilton, nevertheless, also recommended that two original charges be dropped: that Garwood was on unauthorized absence while he was in Vietnam and that he sought to foster disloyalty and insubordination among the prisoners. The charges of desertion, collaboration, and maltreatment still stood.

The court-martial originally had been scheduled to begin in April 1980, but a new lawyer for Garwood, John Lowe, who eventually pushed Foley out of the picture, sought a delay while he developed a new strategy leading to a case for insanity. Garwood's military lawyers, upset with the tactics of Foley the civilian attorney, resigned from the case, leaving open the formation of an all-civilian defense team.

A "White Gook"

After a long series of legal maneuvers, Garwood's lawyers entered an insanity plea on August 1, although opening arguments did not begin until November 13, 1980. After all the intricate legal complexities were boiled down, the case rested on the premise that the trauma of wartime captivity, the isolation, the mental anguish, and the struggle for survival all combined to leave the lowly, uneducated Garwood crazy enough to become a "white gook." If he was crazy, then he could not be held responsible for his actions during his captivity. In rebuttal, the military lawyers simply asked the members of the jury—all Vietnam veterans and all senior officers—to listen to the testimony of the men who were in the jungle and experienced life with Garwood. It was good counsel.

I had begun the testimony as the first witness. I described seeing Garwood carrying a rifle, guarding prisoners, having the freedom to come and go almost at will, spying on the Americans, and participating in the political course. I also mentioned that the camp commander ordered us to treat him with the same deference as expected toward the Vietnamese guards. When asked on cross-examination, I said that he never demanded it and that none of us deferred to him anyway. Robert Lewis, my former crew chief, was called next and said that he had seen Garwood carrying a pistol as well as a rifle, that he lived with the guards, and that he wore a pin bearing the face of Ho Chi Minh on his uniform.

Of the former prisoners who testified during the court-martial, Ike McMillan was probably the most impartial, and so offered the greatest expectations by Garwood's lawyers that he could be led to suggest that their client was just another prisoner doing all he could to save himself. McMillan tried to make certain that his choice of words in describing the years in the jungle were even-handed and not inflammatory in any way. He generally described Garwood's presence in the camps as being more helpful to the Vietnamese in ways that got him special treatment from the cadre and guards rather than being one of the leaders in the camp hierarchy. Lowe, Garwood's lead defense attorney, seemed to sense that McMillan might offer evidence that would be favorable to his client. He bore in on one particular term, "crossover," and suggested that the word itself never was used by the men during their captivity. The lawyer stepped on a land mine:

LOWE: " Now you used the term 'crossover.' Isn't it true that the first time you actually heard those particular words used to mean somebody who switched sides was actually after your release? These were not words that Bobby Garwood himself used, are they? He used some other word like 'cooperate' or something, didn't he?"

McMILLAN: "No, sir."

LOWE: "He didn't. He used the word 'crossover'?"

MCMILLAN: "Crossover, yes sir."

LOWE: "You remember that specifically from twelve years ago as you sit here?"

MCMILLAN: "Crossover or liberated."

LOWE: "Or liberated?"

MCMILLAN: "Right."

LOWE: "It might have been one or the other?"

MCMILLAN: "Those two words were used frequently."

Another serious problem for the accused, as Garwood was referred to during the court-martial, was the recollection of Luis Ortiz-Rivera. The Puerto Rican, who had been in Camp One for a few months when we arrived and was released in early 1968 with Agostos Santos, spoke very little English and was asked very basic questions. His answers were also very simple, basic, and damning. Theresa Wright, the government lawyer, questioned Ortiz-Rivera about his time in the camp with Garwood:

WRIGHT: "What, if any, conversation did you ever have with the accused later regarding his choice to return to the United States?"

ORTIZ-RIVERA: "One time after he was liberated, one of the times that he returned to the compound because he would come and go, we were talking, and I asked him why hadn't he gone, and he said that he couldn't. I asked him then, 'Why don't you go to another country if not the United States?' And he didn't say anything."

WRIGHT: "What, if anything, did the accused ever tell you about why he could not return home?"

ORTIZ-RIVERA: "That same time he told me that he felt better with them, with the Viet Cong, and they treated him better than the U.S. Army."

When it came time for Gus Mehrer to take the stand, the evidence was already piling up, but his recollections were many and truly damaging. His first encounter with Garwood, he said, involved a discussion of events back in America, particularly the antiwar movement and the demonstrations in the cities. Mehrer had told the other prisoners many times of the antiwar demonstrations in the United States and the changed social attitudes, about "free love" on the campuses. When Garwood asked Mehrer about such events, he said, he was interested only in the antiwar movement and the significance of the peace symbol that had gained such widespread popularity. Werner Hellmer, Wright's partner for the government, questioned Mehrer:

HELLMER: "At this first meeting, what, if anything, did the accused show you?"

MEHRER: "During the course of our conversation, he invited me to cross over, or asked me if I

had crossed over, and then invited me to work
with him."

HELLMER: "What, if anything, did the accused
show you?"

MEHRER: "He had a satchel. He said it contained
leaflets."

From there, Mehrer described a megaphone lying
next to the satchel that corroborated other indications
that Garwood had tried to entice U.S. soldiers to lay
down their arms. He told of Garwood's incessant lec-
tures on Vietnamese history, his teaching him of some
of the language, and his telling him that he was the
equivalent of a first lieutenant in the NLF. He described several items that Garwood had in his possession: a photograph of a Vietnamese woman, a
Vietnamese identification card bearing his name and
personal data, some money, and a watch. Garwood,
Mehrer testified, pressured him to join him and even
allowed him to stay in his hootch for awhile before
kicking him down to the prisoner compound with the
rest of us. That was when we first met him.

Dave Harker, who had been struck and knocked to
the ground by Garwood during the cat incident in
Camp Two, reinforced one of the charges that ultimately brought a guilty verdict. Wright conducted the
questioning:

WRIGHT: "Will you explain in more specific
terms the type blow that he struck, how he did
it, and exactly where he hit you."

HARKER: "As I recall, he hit me with the back of
his hand, I don't know whether it was in a fist
or whether it was open-hand that he hit me, in
the rib. I remember he had a disgusted look
on his face. I turned and looked at him, I
guess it was a normal reaction, when he hit
me. And he made the statement, I don't think
it was addressed specifically to me, but made
the statement, something to the effect that
'you're gonna have to pay for what happened
to Russ,' which I found rather ironic."

WRIGHT: "Did it hurt you when he hit you?"

HARKER: "I was more afraid of what my captors
were going to do. I don't . . . you know, hurt?
It probably offended me more than anything
that one of my fellow Americans would strike
me."

In addition to those of us who had testified at the
Article Thirty-Two hearing, "Doc" Kushner appeared
in a dark pin-striped suit and in his articulate, au-
thoritative presentation reinforced the accounts of the
other prisoners. Kushner, who had suffered as much
as anyone in the camps and yet performed tremendous
feats of courage to keep us going, had no undying
love for the military and certainly was opposed to the
conduct of the war. But he knew who was on the
prisoners' side and who wasn't. Hellmer conducted
the direct questioning of Kushner, part of which fol-
lows from excerpts from his testimony.

HELLMER: "Dr. Kushner, what time, if any, did you ever observe the accused acting as a guard for prisoners?"

KUSHNER: "On many occasions. Not one, not two, but many occasions he functioned as a guard in that he carried a weapon, and he went with the prisoners on forays outside the camp to get food or this vegetable, this tuberous plant that we called *manioc*."

HELLMER: "Sir, getting to another area now, what, if anything, did the accused ever tell you concerning the rank that he held?"

KUSHNER: "He told me that he was a first lieutenant in the NVA army."

HELLMER: "Can you recall the circumstances behind this at all?"

KUSHNER: "No."

HELLMER: "Sir, what, if anything, did the accused ever relate to you concerning broadcasts to American troops?"

KUSHNER: "There was a time in the fall of 1968, when he said he was going to be leaving to go down to the plains to make announcements, broadcasts to American troops."

HELLMER: "Did he tell you what the nature of the broadcasts were to be?"

KUSHNER: "They were to be propaganda broadcasts. He didn't specifically go into what he was going to say."

HELLMER: "What, if any, discussions did you ever have with PFC Garwood concerning his opportunity to be released?"

KUSHNER: "Well, I talked to PFC Garwood hundreds of times during my contact with him, and on several of these occasions he had told me about his release."

HELLMER: "What did he tell you about his release?"

KUSHNER: "He told me two versions. Version number one was that he had struck a deal with the Vietnamese and that they had agreed to release him, and in return he would work with them for several months or for a short period of time, at the end of which he would be repatriated home. Okay, version number two—oh, and they had not kept their bargain and that after he had worked for them for this short period of time he was not repatriated, and he was just continuing to work for them. But version number two was that he was morally and philosophically opposed to the war in Vietnam, and he wanted to stay and help the cause."

HELLMER: "What, if any, reaction did you ever observe PFC Garwood have as a result of Grissett's death?"

KUSHNER: "Grissett died on the night of 2 December 1968, in my arms, and Garwood shortly or immediately came down after he had died and appeared to be deeply moved by

the event of Grissett's death and said, 'I told
Grissett to follow me and he followed Eisenbraun. I told him if he followed me, he would
live. He followed Eisenbraun.' "

Our testimony was followed by professional find-
ings of several psychological experts. The four who
testified for the defense portrayed Garwood as a man
shaped by his captors into a different person, a man
not in complete control of his mental faculties. Lowe,
the lawyer for Garwood, did not directly try to refute
the facts that we had presented but sought instead to
make the case that his client's complicity in the actions he was accused of was a matter of proportion
and degree in his efforts to survive. He simply was
not mentally responsible because he was struggling to
survive in the same coercive environment as everyone
else. The prosecution lawyer challenged the insanity
defense as an "orchestrated smoke screen."

Garwood Found Guilty

By late January 1981, the judge in the trial, Col. R. E.
Switzer, dismissed more of the charges for lack of
evidence—desertion, solicitation by using a bullhorn
to encourage U.S. troops to refuse to fight, and verbal
abuse of Richard "Top" Williams. The trial pressed
on. After grueling direct and cross-examination, the
attorneys gave their summation arguments on February 2, 1981, and three days later, the jury rendered its
guilty verdict: for serving as an interpreter during the
political course; for informing on the prisoners to the
captors; for interrogating prisoners about military
matters, including plans for escape; for participating

in the indoctrination of prisoners during the political course and suggesting that they defect to the enemy; for serving as a guard; and for simple assault, the striking of Harker during the camp cat incident.

Then, after dramatic arguments by attorneys for both sides, the punishment phase went back to the jury. Prosecutor Wright closed by asking the members of the jury how it must have felt to watch a fellow American turn on them. Lowe countered that Garwood had suffered enough, first from his fourteen years in Vietnam and then from the ignominy of being charged with misconduct when several hundred returnees in Operation Homecoming not only were not prosecuted for their violations of the code of conduct but also were granted amnesty.

The jury took less than an hour to impose what was little more than a slap on the wrist, considering that Garwood came into the court-martial with the possibility of receiving a death sentence or life imprisonment. He was reduced to the lowest rank, given a dishonorable discharge, and required to forfeit pay and allowances, applied only to the week between conviction and sentencing.

I thought that was enough. The punishment was substantial and absolutely justified for the accumulation of things that Garwood had done. One incident, taken in isolation from the others, would not seem to be so serious, but taken together in the pattern of his actions and their consequences, his behavior was an affront to decency. I've often thought about the day that I crossed paths with him while on the way to the water cooler. "Why didn't you just come clean, Bobby?" I wanted to say to him. He screwed up. I understand he was a kid in 1965, when he was probably captured, but after that he basically screwed up. If he had just stood up and said, "I fucked up," and had come home admitting his mistakes and professing sorrow for his actions, I probably never would have testified against him. I had promised Hammond in the jungle that I would do all I could to make sure that the world learned the truth about him, but I didn't harbor any hate.

Today, I still don't look back at Garwood as a traitor but as a crossover, someone who sells out his fellow prisoners, whereas a traitor sells out his country. A lot of mistakes were made by the POWs in the jungle camps of Vietnam. None of us except Bobby Garwood, though, crossed over to the side of the enemy despite our hardships. Certainly, most of us to one extent or another found ourselves forced into writing statements, and Kushner did make a few broadcasts, but we always did it in a way that tried to hedge or fall just short of being disloyal or causing harm to our country. In the jungle, Garwood's rationale was, "I'm going to take care of me," and he never took into account the effect on the lives and minds of the other Americans.

During the court-martial, my anger was not so much directed at Garwood—to tell the truth, I really pitied him—but at the general tenor of the country, especially the lawyers in the case. Of course, their job was to be an advocate in an adversarial proceeding, but they portrayed him as someone who didn't do anything different from the rest of us, which was patently absurd. The image they drew was of a hapless pack mule used by the Vietnamese to do their will. I lived with him for eighteen brutal months—months that were fatal to many of my comrades—and I know what the difference was between him and the rest of us. We were prisoners. He might have been one at some point, but not while I knew him.

For those of us jungle prisoners who went to Camp Lejeune to testify to what we had seen and endured, it was a journey that took us back to our misery. The Bobby Garwood court-martial put a part of history to rest, yet it also forced many of us to return to the memories of that horrid experience. Many of the questions surrounding Garwood's capture and fourteen years in Vietnam remain unanswered to this day. In a way, his case is a metaphor for the U.S. role in Vietnam. When it was over, too many questions remained unanswered.

They Died Needlessly

After twenty-five years of reflection, I cannot escape the belief that not only did so many valiant Americans die needlessly because of a flawed prosecution of what at one time had been a justifiable war, but also that so many needlessly suffered the horrors of captivity in the Vietnam jungle. Only Garwood can answer the question about what happened to him during all those years.

I know from personal experience, though, that some of the things that he has claimed happened are simply not true. Maybe to some people, after all this time, it really doesn't matter. War is terrible and ugly, they may say, and bad things happen to good people. But the worst is betrayal. You expect your enemy to try to kill or wound you or to capture you, but you never expect your own to turn on you and betray you.

The covenant between a nation and the people it

sends into war obliges that nation to do all within its power to return home those servicemen captured in the line of duty. The other side of the bargain requires each serviceman, to the fullest extent humanly possible, to keep the faith not only with the ideals of the country he fought to defend but also, if captured, with the other prisoners who share his fate. Garwood failed the test of keeping the faith. In some ways, what he endured was as bad as what the rest of us went through, maybe even worse. He just made up his mind that he wasn't going to do that anymore. We suffered the consequences of that decision, and eventually, even though it took almost a decade and a half, he suffered it too.

13
A Cynical Attitude

One of the most gratifying experiences of those months after I had returned home from Vietnam was receiving invitations to speak to school assemblies and civic clubs. Mostly I talked about a few of the events during my captivity. If the audience was schoolchildren, I would concentrate on stories that I thought they would understand and enjoy, so naturally I avoided describing gruesome details of the effects that the diseases had on our bodies or the mental torture of watching friends die. I spoke in general terms of how we had only a little food to eat and that it was a lot worse than the lunches they ate in their cafeterias. The kids got a kick out of that that little joke, but I never was sure the teachers and principals did. I also told them how well the American people had treated me after I came home from the long years that I was in the camps and prisons, and I emphasized how precious freedom had become to me.

For the older students, in high schools and colleges, I talked more about how terrible the war was in a faraway place that most of us never really understood. I was careful not to be publicly critical of how the government conducted the war. But I tried not to pull any punches about how difficult and even sad it was to be involved in something that caused so many brave men to be killed and wounded as well as to be captured and to endure the pain and hardship of being a POW.

Some Had Tough Questions

Many times, students would ask questions after I had made my presentation, but they usually just asked for more details of what it was like to be in the war and to be captured by the Vietnamese. The talks I gave to civic groups, though, produced more penetrating questions. Some of the inquiries were asked in such a way that required a political viewpoint, and those I avoided. After all, I was still a member of the armed forces, and as an official representative I felt obligated to keep my personal political views to myself. But one question kept coming up over and over, and with the adult audiences it became one of the most prominent topics I was asked about: *Were any POWs left behind?* My stock answer, which I considered a reasonable conclusion and not just a political opinion, was of course men were left behind. I had seen the warrant officer on the Ho Chi Minh trail in Laos during my march to North Vietnam, and the debriefers satisfied me that they had no information on him. We had scoured hundreds of photographs in books that represented the government's store of known missing men. The man's picture was not there. He was just as alive as I was, standing not more than ten feet away from me, and he was alive when his guards hastily moved him away from me when they were aware I had seen him.

I knew of the conversations between cell walls in the Hanoi prison, where the B-52 pilots were nursing men who had suffered lost arms and legs. I had seen the photograph in the Hanoi newspaper showing other men with missing limbs. Apparently, the military doctors at the hospital in Manila expected many such wounded men to need special care at their first stop during Operation Homecoming. A large number of hospital rooms had been set aside at Clark Air Force Base to receive patients with massive injuries, but all 591 men released in early 1973—all that both the United States and Vietnam officially reported as having been in POW status—were in relatively decent health. There were no amputees or servicemen with massive injuries normally associated with ejecting from a jet aircraft, nor were there any cases of serious burns also common with pilots of planes shot down by missiles or antiaircraft fire. So yes, I said, I believed that men were still being held prisoner by the Vietnamese. I couldn't be 100 percent certain, but I was 99 percent certain.

Maybe They Were Overlooked

Privately, I assumed that the discrepancy was just another military oversight, or blunder, possibly understandable in the confusing rush to get the POWs out of Vietnam as soon as possible. People just got in too big a hurry, I thought at first, and some men were overlooked, possibly those being held in prisons remote from Hanoi or even some who still had not yet emerged from the isolated jungle camps.

As I was to learn later, the number of men released was far below what had been estimated and expected by high-level Pentagon officials, as many as several hundred below. No one who was missing in Laos was ever returned, and the government knew of more than three hundred servicemen last known to be held in Laos when the war ended. I personally saw one of them. But the Operation Homecoming show had to go on, and it played to great fanfare before a country tremendously relieved that the United States was finally leaving Vietnam.

In September 1973, after more than five months of enjoying life and a good deal of recognition, I was asked to be part of a program at a college in Ocean County, New Jersey, not far from my parents' home. The college had planned a discussion of the Vietnam War and invited a couple of servicemen who were from the area to relate their experiences and participate in a public discussion with the audience that gathered in the college auditorium. Most of them came because of their interest in U.S. servicemen still missing in action. I was joined on the stage by an air force colonel who was assigned to the Pentagon.

The two of us gave our respective viewpoints of Vietnam, his from that of a fighter pilot and mine from that of a jungle prisoner. We each gave a five-minute synopsis of our experiences and then opened the floor to questions. Eventually, someone brought up the issue of men who were missing. *Were they left?* the questioner asked. I answered first. "Sure," I said. "Absolutely, I believe they were." The colonel became visibly agitated. As the defender of official policy, he could not allow the assertion to stand. "Frank," he said, "I like you personally, but this is wrong to give people false hope."

The Colonel Was Offended

The audience may not have come to the program expecting a vigorous pro-con discussion of a lively, controversial issue, but that's what they got. I responded to my counterpart's comment that I had seen the chopper pilot in Laos and then recounted the discussions in the prison about the wounded B-52 pilots and how none of them came back during Operation Homecoming. He clearly took offense and then dismissed my remarks, as if I were well-meaning but naive, assuring the audience that the U.S. government would never leave Americans behind. I noticed that he seemed to be taking notes, but only while I was speaking.

A couple of weeks later, I received a call from a colonel in the Pentagon who told me politely but firmly that he understood that I was making public statements that men were left behind in Vietnam. I affirmed that I had but then explained to him the reasons for my observations. After a long, silent pause, he said, "Look, we know we left people back there. We're doing everything we can to get them back, but your talking about it doesn't help us get them back." He also told me that the issue posed a very delicate political situation and asked if I expected the United States to go back to war over it. "Sir," I said, "I'd go."

I took the colonel's counsel to heart, but as I was invited to make more speaking engagements, the sub-

ject kept coming up. I told what I believed to be the
truth, that I thought men had been left behind. Several
months later, I received another call, this time from a
brigadier general in the Pentagon. The general gave
me a sterner, unmistakable warning. "Do you want to
stay in the military?" he asked gruffly and then continued without waiting for my response. "Then stop
talking about the MIA issue." I had planned to make
a career of the military, so I followed his advice. I
tucked the issue in the back of my mind and decided
to leave well enough alone. I have been uncomfort-
able and ashamed of that decision ever since.

Not everyone, of course, agreed to leave it well
enough alone. Almost as soon as the United States
ended its role in the war, the questions, especially
from family members, began to arise as to whether
all the men came home. Henry Kissinger, who led the
U.S. delegation at the Paris peace talks to negotiate
an end to the war, knew as soon as the North Vietnamese handed over the list of the men it reported to
have in captivity that the list was incomplete. Not
only did the list fail to include men the United States
knew from photographic proof to have been in cus-
tody of the Vietnamese, but many prisoners known
by U.S. officials to have been captured and held in
Laos failed to appear on the list as well. Air Force
Gen. Eugene Tighe, who later became the head of the
Defense Intelligence Agency, said that the discovery
left U.S. intelligence agents in a state of "shock and
sadness."

Kissinger, though, should not have been terribly
surprised. Throughout the exhausting negotiations in
Paris, the one consistent theme repeated many times
by the Vietnamese was the connection between re-

lease of prisoners and the payment of reparations by the United States to "heal the wounds of war."

Hanoi's negotiators, who had driven the Americans to their wits' end with frustrating demands for concessions—even over the shape of the table when the talks began—made clear that they would not separate the issue of reparations from the release of American prisoners. Kissinger used every ounce of his considerable diplomatic cunning to separate the linkage between the two, but the Vietnamese were unbending. For them, the linkage was essential and nonnegotiable. In short, if the United States wanted its POWs back, it would have to pay ransom, reparations, reconstruction assistance, or whatever other term it chose to use.

Nor should Kissinger have been surprised by the matter of using POWs for political leverage. Holding prisoners as barter to exchange for future political or material considerations is almost as old as history itself. But it had become an article of faith under Marxism-Leninism, beginning with the Bolshevik Revolution. After World War II, more than twenty thousand American POWs in Nazi prison camps in Poland were "liberated" by advancing Soviet troops and were never heard from again. The Allied command had begged Gen. George C. Marshall to allow them to advance in force to seize the prisons and get the prisoners out, but Marshall refused so as to avoid an extension of the war against the Soviets after a war-weary nation had defeated the Axis.

American POWs from the Korean War were also unaccounted for after the 1953 armistice, and an unknown number, according to U.S. intelligence analysts, were shipped to China and the Soviet Union. By 1955, we have only recently learned, President

Dwight D. Eisenhower knew that some prisoners had been kept in North Korea and in some Chinese camps, and he was presented intelligence reports indicating that eight hundred had been sent by train to Siberia. Knowing that the Soviets never would acknowledge holding the prisoners, much less release them, Eisenhower, out of concern for their families, chose not to make the report public. For nearly forty years that ugly secret was withheld from the public, and the fate of some eight thousand Korean War POWs is still unknown.

The Vietnamese, heirs to the ideology, strategy, and tactics of other communist regimes, followed suit in dealing with the prisoner issue after their colonial war against France. After the fall of Dien Bien Phu in 1954, some five thousand French soldiers and foreign legionnaires were held for years in captivity, according to a 1965 report by the Rand Corporation. A subsequent CIA report told of Moroccans still returning home in the early 1970s, and some partially declassified 1983 State Department telegrams indicated that some French POWs were being secretly returned during the 1980s.

Kissinger Knew of Report

Kissinger was very much familiar with such documentation, especially the Rand report, which suggested that American policy in Southeast Asia should anticipate the exploitation of captured Americans for political and economic concessions. The Rand report, commissioned by the government, carefully documented the likely scenario that would play out if an American escalation of its involvement in the war resulted in introducing more soldiers into harm's way. The nettlesome problem of having to deal with a rising number of prisoners was not just possible, it was inevitable. In addition, according to Rand, the United States should also anticipate paying ransom, probably in the guise of reconstruction aid or some other diplomatically acceptable euphemism, in exchange for the release of prisoners. The 1965 report was prophetic.

Unfortunately, U.S. policymakers resorted to historical precedent in considering the diplomatic and political implications of such a problem during the Cold War. An internal memorandum written by Pentagon analyst James Kelleher in 1955 argued that the United States was probably going to be involved in several limited wars such as Korea. If so, he wrote, then the issue of POWs "becomes almost a philosophical one. If we are 'at war,' cold, hot, or otherwise, casualties and losses must be expected, and perhaps we must learn to live with this type of thing. If we are in for fifty years of peripheral 'firefights' we may be forced to adopt a rather cynical attitude on this for political reasons."

Two years later, in 1957, the Pentagon adopted the policy contained in a classified paper, most likely written by a young academician named Henry Kissinger, as its blueprint for conducting limited wars of the future. The major powers could not afford to wage nuclear war against each other, so they would seek geopolitical advantage through proxy wars. The limited nature of any future such U.S. involvement in a land war, the report said, would leave the territory in question out of U.S. control at the conflict's conclusion. Therefore, we would not know whether all

American POWs had been released—as happened in Korea and, years later, in Vietnam. Under the new policy of "cynical thinking," we would just have to live with it and find a way to work around it. In other words, some disposable assets might have to be written off as combat losses.

Under Incredible Pressure

Such was the intellectual framework that Kissinger took to the Paris peace negotiations. In fairness, he was under incredible pressure by the time the talks began to reach critical stages in mid-1972. Antiwar sentiment was building to almost fever pitch at home, and it was gaining momentum with the ascendance of Senator McGovern as the antiwar challenger to President Nixon.

Kissinger needed to sign a deal that would allow the greatest possible face-saving, but the Vietnamese were hard bargainers. They were holding valuable collateral in their prisons, and U.S. intelligence agents knew from their sources as early as 1971 that hundreds more prisoners were under Hanoi's control than the Vietnamese were admitting in the Paris negotiations. The CIA that year had interviewed a highly credible defector, Vietnamese mortician Dr. Dang Tan, who said that five hundred or more American prisoners not named in Paris were being held secretly. He also told U.S. agents that "some may never be released."

CIA Director Richard Helms notified Kissinger through a secret cable about Tan on May 10, 1971, warning him that Vietnam would probably use the POWs "in blackmailing the U.S.A." Further supporting the probability that a large group of Americans was being held secretly was a briefing delivered on Sept. 15, 1972 to the Soviet Central Committee of the Communist Party by NVA Lt. Gen. Tran Van Quang. He told the Soviets that 1,205 Americans had been captured in Vietnam, Cambodia, and Laos—more than double the number identified and released at Operation Homecoming. The transcript of the general's report did not surface until Harvard professor Dr. Steven Morris happened upon it in Moscow while he was doing unrelated research in archives of the former Soviet Union in 1992.

In their book, *The Men We Left Behind*, Jim Sanders and Mark Sauter wrote that about the time of the Helms memo, Kissinger agreed to share last-minute lists of prisoners with the Vietnamese, without any prior assurances that all prisoners held under the control of North Vietnam would be on the list. In other words, Kissinger was to trust them to do what nothing in their recent history would justify. As the Rand report predicted, Kissinger soon found himself with a hostage crisis on his hands. To elude the trap set for him, Kissinger adopted a tough posture with the Vietnamese, in effect telling them that other policy considerations for the United States were far more compelling than the POWs. If they wanted to hold prisoners, he said, that was their business, but America would simply abandon the negotiations and leave the North Vietnamese with no further bargaining leverage. Hanoi didn't fall for the bluff because it wasn't credible—unless Kissinger himself was really willing to betray the POWs. Public pressure in America was then building intensely for an end to the war, and the prisoners' release had become inextricably connected with that outcome.

Sanders's and Sauter's meticulous documentation from official declassified cables and other records demonstrates that Kissinger desperately tried to break the linkage between POWs and ransom. During secret negotiations in September 1972, he was virtually begging his counterpart, Le Duc Tho, to assure the Americans that Vietnam would vouch for all prisoners in Southeast Asia, including Cambodia and Laos. The Vietnamese refused to budge, although the language in the documents was masterfully veiled, meandering, and ambiguous. Any consideration of prisoners in Cambodia or Laos would have to be achieved separately "in accordance with the sovereignty" of those governments. That is, the United States would have to enter separate, protracted negotiations with those two countries in talks similar to the ordeal in Paris— clearly an evasive tactic because Hanoi dictated virtually every aspect of political and military action among the three countries, especially control of American prisoners. In other words, only when U.S. reparations had been paid to Vietnam would Hanoi begin to take up the POW issue. Kissinger and Nixon cratered and accepted the agreement, after sending the Vietnamese a "secret" letter assuring payment of more than $4 billion in reconstruction aid and other "unconditional" assistance. It was never paid because Laos never released the prisoners that the State Department and National Security Council—but not Kissinger—knew were still being held. The "deal" stalemated.

By March, the U.S. troop withdrawal from Vietnam halted, and some officials recommended hostile actions against Laos. But Nixon and his advisers in Washington, feeling the first waves of heat from a developing Watergate scandal and unwilling to prolong the withdrawal from Southeast Asia, summarily declared that all the prisoners had been returned, and anyone who was still missing was dead. That became the official U.S. policy, and the Pentagon followed the policy from that point on with unyielding obedience.

A Painful Dilemma

The history of the "cynical attitude" is crucial to understanding the painful dilemma of the American POWs from previous wars, especially Korea and Vietnam. That is not to say that the issue died. The flood of Vietnamese refugees after the fall of Saigon in April 1975 poured countless reports into the hands of U.S. intelligence analysts of living American prisoners still being held in Vietnam. True, many of the refugees who were part of the flood of "boat people" escaping Hanoi's control of the country fabricated stories in hopes that their reports of live American POWs would result in favorable treatment, even assistance in emigrating from the refugee camps in Thailand to the United States. Many others, though, passed exhaustive lie-detector tests to support their claims of live sightings.

U.S. officials charged with accounting for missing servicemen after the war kept meticulous files on the live-sighting reports, some of them even noted as being "highly credible," but they devoted far more time and resources attempting to discredit them than in following up on the leads. Several congressional investigations made ineffectual efforts to determine whether servicemen were still in captivity, but none until 1991 did more than scratch the surface, relying instead on the self-serving defense by the Pentagon that all the men were dead.

In the meantime, Vietnam was in an economic shambles after the war. Hanoi had expected billions of dollars in reparations and reconstruction aid, but political inertia won the day in Washington. The money was not forthcoming because Congress, unaware of Nixon's secret, "unconditional" offer of $4 billion and angered by the brutal treatment of the men who had returned, voted overwhelmingly to reject any aid for Vietnam. Yet evidence of living prisoners continued for years to seep quietly out of Southeast Asia, some from refugees and some from official intelligence sources, including communications intercepts and satellite imagery.

Even Bobby Garwood came home telling of live Americans he had seen between 1973 and 1978. According to him, as soon as he arrived from Hanoi to board the plane in Bangkok that returned him to the United States in March of 1979, he tried to tell his military escorts that he had seen several American prisoners, but he was read his rights and told to say nothing. In 1985, he wrote a letter to a congressional subcommittee and asked to testify in public that he had seen fifty to sixty American prisoners and that they wanted to come home. Much of what Garwood said while I knew him in the jungle was not true, but some of it was. Because he was an opportunist then, I do not think that his comments on the issue are the most reliable indicator of what the truth may be. His assertions, however, should not be summarily dismissed.

But Jerry Mooney, a crypto-linguist with the National Security Agency, sought for years to convince congressional committees that he had listened to conversations of Vietnamese guards supervising the movement of American prisoners during the war and after the U.S. withdrawal, tracking the exact locations of their progress within Vietnam and also monitoring the movements of some who boarded aircraft apparently destined, Mooney said, for China and the Soviet Union.

A Clear Signal

Such official signal-intercept surveillance was continuing at least three years after Operation Homecoming. Indeed, a U.S. satellite image taken in June 1992 of the Dong Mang prison in northern Vietnam showed a man-made signal stamped out in the grass: GX 2527. Pentagon analysts tried to argue that the image was a "photographic anomaly," but the combination of letters and digits matched the unique authenticator code of Peter Richard Matthes, the copilot of a C-130 transport shot down in Laos in November of 1969 and still listed as missing in action at the time the satellite snapped the picture. Each pilot was issued such a unique code so that he could radio a rescue team that he was a downed U.S. pilot. Mother Nature may have been dabbling with creative touches to the terrain, but the coincidence of the sudden appearance of a unique code associated with an American pilot missing for twenty-two years is astonishing. Even more astonishing was the fact that the location of the image was adjacent to a prison. Unfortunately, the Pentagon does not appear to have investigated the mysterious "coincidence."

Also in 1992, Le Quang Khai defected to the United States, or tried to. After years of advancing through the Vietnamese Foreign Ministry, Khai had been enrolled at Columbia University to do graduate work. One of the most senior Vietnamese officials ever to defect to the United States, he reported that it was "common knowledge" within the Vietnamese government that U.S. POWs had been held back after the war, according to Sanders and Sauter in *The Men We Left Behind*. For this revelation, Khai was issued his deportation notice by the U.S. government.

The history of the POW/MIA issue is as murky as it is distasteful. For nearly three decades, whether through willful, orchestrated evasion or through simple bureaucratic indifference and inertia, the issue has virtually disappeared into an official black hole. Maybe the questions about what happened to the men who were left behind will never be answered. Army Col. Millard A. "Mike" Peck, former head of the Office of POW/MIA in the Defense Intelligence Agency, wrote in his resignation letter in 1991, after blasting the agency's "mindset to debunk," that the government's feeble attempts to account for missing men may never have been an honest effort in the first place. That mindset continued when a new Senate select committee was formed in 1991 to conduct the most exhaustive investigation ever into the issue. I watched those proceedings, and at first believed that finally the lid would be pried open and the truth would be exposed. Like so many others, though, I watched in disbelief and anger at the committee's efforts to disprove, rather than prove, in the face of enormous amounts of evidence, that men not only were abandoned after 1973, but that some still could have been held against their will.

The saddest part was how close the committee had come so many times to forcing evidence out of the musty secret files of the Pentagon and intelligence agencies only to refuse at a critical time to invoke its subpoena power or to fail to call critical witnesses who had firsthand knowledge of POWs.

I was contacted by the committee staff during the early phases of the inquiry and replied that I would eagerly accept the opportunity to reveal my experiences, especially regarding those men I knew had not returned. I never heard from the committee again. My testimony would not have been critical to the outcome, but it would have been a piece of the puzzle. I became convinced that the vast majority of the senators on the committee had decided that one last grand charade was necessary before burying the issue once and for all. Any dispassionate reading of its huge, evasive report cannot help but support that conclusion.

The "Cynical Attitude"

What is most troubling about this century's history of American prisoners of war is the "cynical attitude" adopted as unofficial policy more than forty years ago. I learned from cruel experience that there were limits to the value placed by the government on men who fell into the enemy's hands. The miracles of technology were wonders to behold as the most powerful military force in the history of the world went to war with a small Asian country half a world away. Unfortunately, the United States became mesmerized by its technology and lulled into an infatuation with its awesome machines. This occurred to the extent that the human beings caught up in that war too often became abstractions in the war rooms of the generals and politicians who were far removed from the slaughter and suffering. At the highest levels, the cost in blood and treasure became secondary to grand designs, majestic theories, and a worship of statistical probabilities. The men who were killed or wounded or who spent years of physical agony and mental torment in the putrid, debilitating jungle camps and prisons too often became the objects of a "cynical attitude."

The technology could sense us, and watch us, and even come close enough to us that we dared to hope that our faith had been sustained, that our comrades would retrieve us from the nightmare of our captivity. But it seemed that there were limits that those who controlled the technology would adhere to rather than snatch us back to freedom. They used their marvelous instruments to watch us closely and for a long time— but from a distance.

Amazing Capabilities

As I lay in the muck of a rice paddy covered by a shroud of thick fog, a ghostly white helicopter appeared mysteriously from nowhere in the predawn darkness of the day I was captured. That chopper, I knew, possessed capabilities that were beyond my imagination. I was bewildered at its presence, aware that no normal helicopter could fly in those conditions, and I was frustrated by the inability of the crew to see me just a few feet directly beneath them. If they had capabilities to venture unscathed into such a precarious position, didn't they also have some heat- or odor-sensing device on board to make the trip worthwhile?

Once I had been captured and taken into the jungle camps, someone had to know exactly where the prisoners were. Patterns of artillery fire were mathematically systematic. The batteries on the distant fire bases charted harassment and interdiction rounds—H&I—to explode in longitudinal and latitudinal patterns around their target areas. I could hear the H&I rounds "walking" toward the camp, each round coming progressively closer until the next round should have landed right in the camp. Then there would be a momentary pause, and the "walking" explosions would continue on the other side. With the exception of one errant round that landed just beyond the prisoners' compound in Camp Four, the artillery seemed to be aimed to deliberately miss the prisoners. Nor did any air strikes hit the camps, although the fighters and B-52s dumped high-explosive bombs all around us. Someone knew where we were.

One bright, moonlit night in late January 1971, I peered through an opening in the jungle canopy. As I gazed upward, an almost imperceptible shadow crept over me and a low, droning noise passed overhead. In a moment, it was gone. Two or three days later, the afternoon sky was filled with American helicopters spiraling downward toward the camp in a combat assault formation. One came close, so incredibly close that I saw the black face of an infantry captain. He knew exactly where we were, and for whatever reason, he and the soldiers with him never came to get me out.

As I limped in pain along the Ho Chi Minh trail, someone was there keeping an eye on me. From somewhere behind the concealment of jungle foliage, a camera captured my image, a curious, unrecognizable image that was to stare me in the face more than two years later after I had returned home. Someone knew where I was.

For three years, I was held in four jungle camps, each shrouded by the central highland forests that I thought were hiding me from the rest of the world. I felt swallowed up, lost, never sure exactly where I was. Yet I returned home to see the photographic evidence— each picture taken during the times that I was in each of the camps—that someone knew where I was.

Haunting Questions

Recently, Chuck Carlock, one of my comrades who was a gunship pilot with the Firebirds, received a letter from retired Army Sgt. Lawrence E. Manton, who served in Vietnam in 1967–68. Manton had written to comment on Carlock's wartime memoir, *Firebirds*, published in 1995, and his letter recalled in some detail several incidents that he had experienced as an infantryman during his tour of duty. He also asked whether Carlock could answer some questions that had haunted him for more than thirty years.

"There are some questions I am curious about that maybe you could answer if you ever find the time," Manton wrote. "I have always been in a quandary why the U.S. Army didn't make more of a concerted effort to get some of our POWs back. I know in the book *Survivors* Anton was almost shot up by some choppers that got so close to them they could almost see the whites of their eyes. Yet there never seemed to be any follow-up. I find it hard to believe that those chopper pilots didn't relay that info back."

Manton had been working with a long-range reconnaissance patrol in the Que Son Valley at the time I was shot down and captured on Jan. 5–6, 1968. He had been attached to Alpha Company of the 196th Light Infantry Brigade, the grunts that our gunships were trying to cover when I was shot down, but he was away on a recon mission when they were overrun. A few weeks later, he was on a patrol in the same area shortly after Bravo Company had been hit hard and overrun. His patrol spotted a small group of people, two of them black, walking south of the Thu Bon River and near the village of Hiep Duc, an area south and west of my shoot-down. James Daly and Willie Watkins had been captured after the ambush of Bravo Company and eventually came into Camp Two with us.

"Two of the people were black and that would coincide with the POWs from the mortar platoon taken when B Company was mauled," Manton wrote to Carlock. "We wanted to go in the minute that we heard about it, but no one would give us the green light. I found it interesting that they never let us go south of the Thu Bon River. It was like some kind of sanctuary that we weren't allowed to go in."

I have since learned that all four of the jungle camps where I was held were beyond the Thu Bon River. If Manton is correct, then LRRP teams whose missions were to penetrate enemy areas of operations were explicitly ordered to stay out of a zone where known prison camps were holding American POWs. They were known, because I saw the aerial photographs taken by U.S. reconnaissance planes while I was in each one.

There Are Some Answers

Only within the last year did I discover at least some of the answers to why my fellow prisoners and I were never rescued from the jungle camps. A person I know, and consider to be an unimpeachable source, worked after his Vietnam tour in the Pentagon and had access to high-level defense intelligence data and became aware of top-secret operations during the war. I am respecting his understandable request for anonymity, although a good deal is generally known publicly about the Studies and Observations Group, or SOG, which was a joint-service, high-command unconventional warfare task force engaged in highly secret operations throughout Southeast Asia.

Composed mostly of members of the Army Special Forces and Navy Seals, as well as about eight thousand indigenous troops, SOG's five key responsibilities were cross-border operations into Laos and Cambodia; organizing resistance in North Vietnam; psychological warfare; kidnappings and assassinations; and monitoring POWs. My source told me, "Frank, they didn't get you out because they didn't want to tip the fact that they knew where you were. The NVA would then begin to identify their sources, which included people within the Viet Cong and very likely the NVA structure. They chose not to compromise their sources because the information was more valuable than you were."

In effect, I read that as meaning that we were expendable. If the jungle prisoners had known that their lives dangled by the tiny thread of the official policy of a "cynical attitude," then I have no doubt that the despair from that betrayal would have caused virtually every one of us to die.

We experienced firsthand what the awful toll could be for a person who finally discovered that he no longer had the heart or the will to go on living, because dying was easier. Survival was difficult enough even with the heroic efforts by some of my comrades who refused to let me give up. We endured hardship that at times almost defied the imagination. Most of us are alive today because, deep down, we placed our hope and trust in the belief that someone was searching for us, was seeking a way to lift us out of oblivion, and most of us managed to keep on hoping. We had confidence in the government that had asked us to risk the sweetness of life itself in service to the mission assigned to us because we expected that if we were wounded we would be healed, and if we were captured our country would come after us. Without that sustaining hope, there would have been no reason to go on. Dying would have been its own consolation.

For the last twenty-five years, I have reviewed time and time again that long nightmare. I have pieced together all the individual incidents of my captivity that indicated just how close freedom had been and yet how far away it actually was. I cannot help but wonder why they, whoever they were who had been so near, didn't get me out of there.

In time, I have come to learn that some leaders of my country had adopted a cynical attitude that was beneath the dignity and honor of the United States of America. That is a grave consequence for future generations to consider when young men and women, facing the ultimate test of battles to come, weigh whether their willingness to commit the last full measure of their devotion will be honored in turn by the nation they serve if they are taken as prisoners of war.

Too many of my jungle comrades paid the ultimate price for the prevailing spirit of cynicism during their war. I am heartsick that so many others of us were consigned to a pit of hell that we need not have had to inhabit for as long as we did because someone knew where we were. I am no less heartsick now to ponder the fate of men who may still be far from home, withering away and wondering why their country had forsaken them.

There is no more solemn covenant between a country and those it asks to go into battle than to do all that is humanly possible to bring them home. I was deeply grateful that I came home after five years of imprisonment, but I returned convinced that others were not so fortunate, that their fate had somehow become entrapped in a netherworld of politics, intrigue, and official secrecy where so many questions still reverberate in an unanswering void:

Why is facing the truth such a hard concession?
Why should cynicism prevail over honor?
Why should betrayal prevail over duty?
Why, at last, didn't they get us all out?

It was a war within a war—and it took no prisoners...

COVERT OPS
The CIA's Secret War in Laos

James E. Parker, Jr.

For the first time, veteran James Parker, codename "Mule," reveals the story of the covert war in Laos—a bloody battle that raged behind the face of the Vietnam War. As Parker takes you inside the hell and devastation of war, he provides a first-person account of the people who courageously fought until the bitter end.

(Previously published in hardcover as *Codename Mule*)

AVAILABLE WHEREVER BOOKS ARE SOLD
FROM ST. MARTIN'S PRESS

They go where no one else will go.
They do what no one else will do.
And they're proud to be called ...

TWILIGHT WARRIORS

INSIDE THE WORLD S SPECIAL FORCES

MARTIN C. AROSTEGUI

From deadly Scud hunts in the Gulf War to daring hostage
rescue missions at London's Iranian Embassy, Special
Forces go where no other army would dare—fighting for
their countries and their lives on the world's most dangerous
missions. Now, journalist and counterterrorism expert
Martin C. Arostegui tells their story—a fascinating true
account of bravery, daring, and the ultimate risk.

TWILIGHT WARRIORS
Martin C. Arostegui
0-312-96493-5____$6.99 U.S.

AVAILABLE WHEREVER BOOKS ARE SOLD
ST. MARTIN'S PAPERBACKS